Lesson on Blood Circulation

Biology 4th Grade

Children's Biology Books

BABY PROFESSOR

EDUCATION KIDS

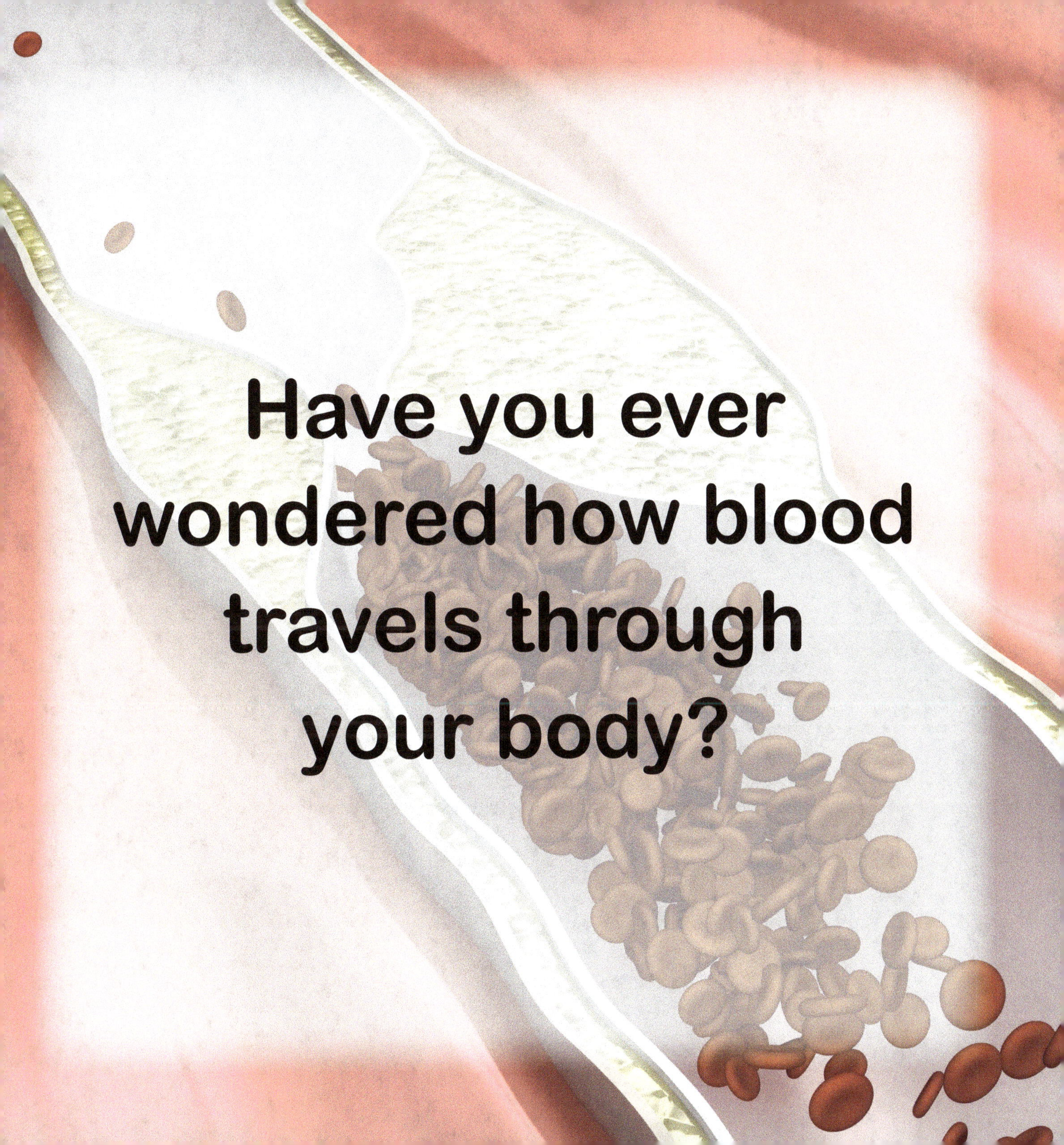

Have you ever wondered how blood travels through your body?

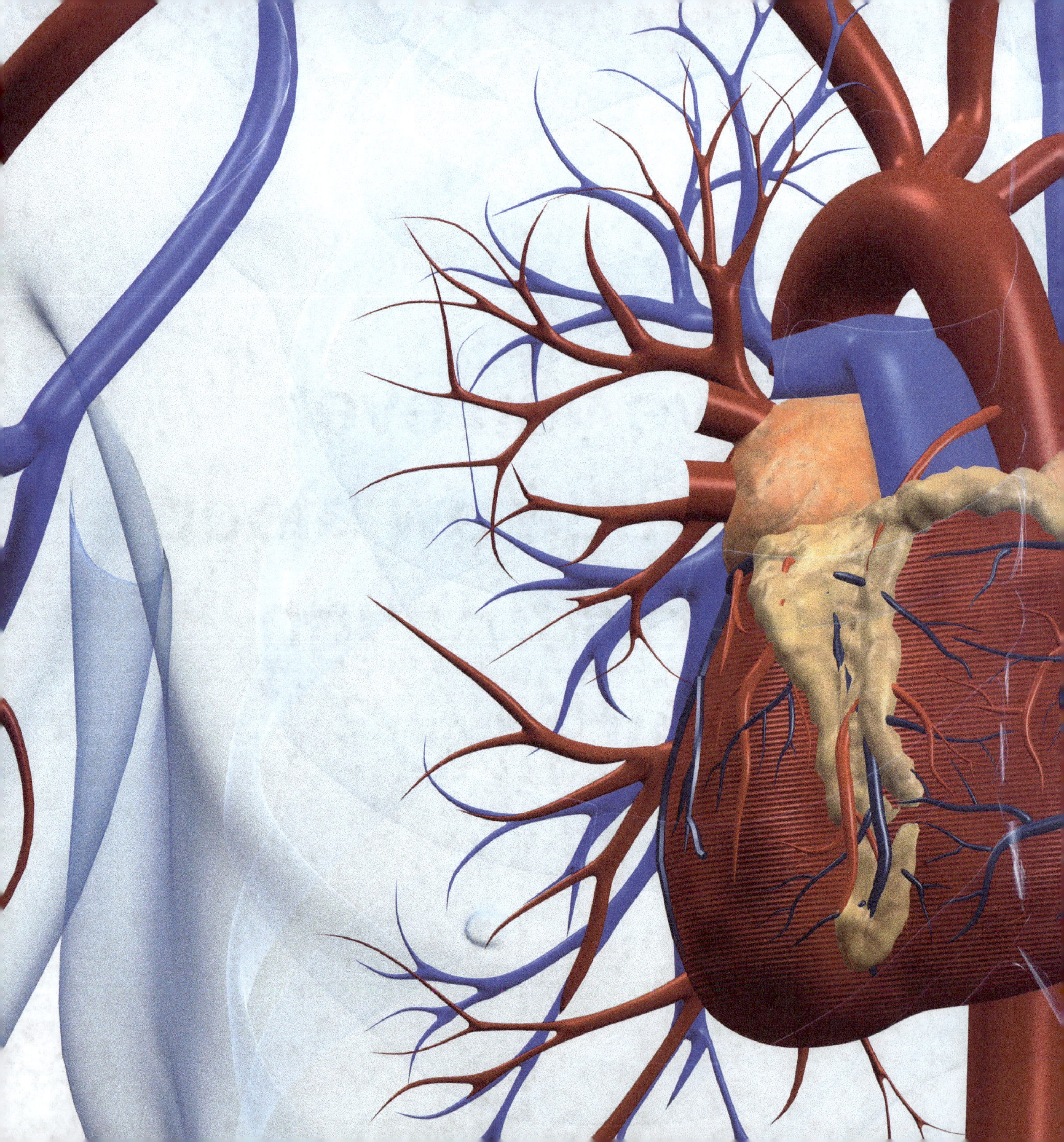

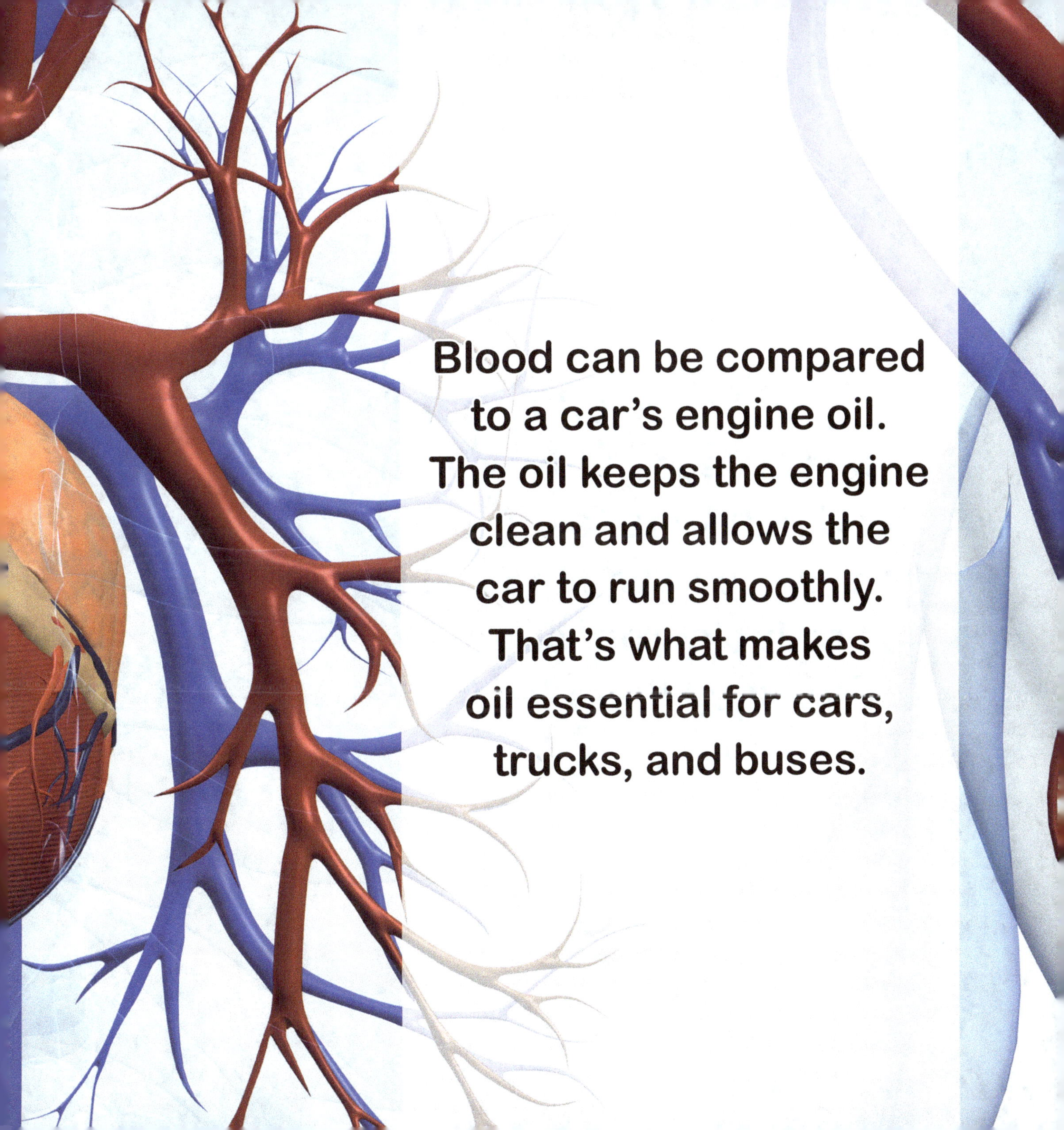

Blood can be compared
to a car's engine oil.
The oil keeps the engine
clean and allows the
car to run smoothly.
That's what makes
oil essential for cars,
trucks, and buses.

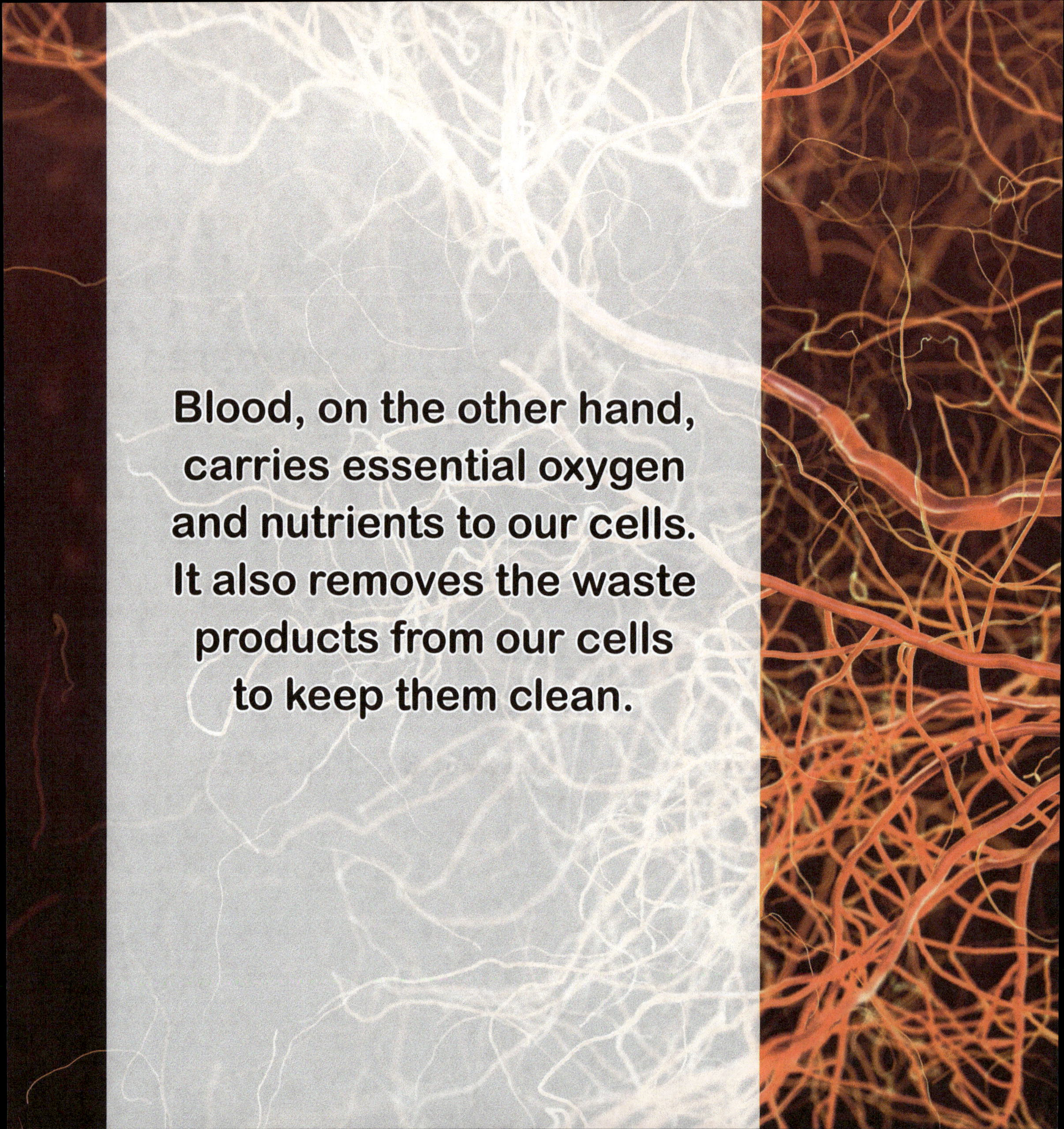
Blood, on the other hand,
carries essential oxygen
and nutrients to our cells.
It also removes the waste
products from our cells
to keep them clean.

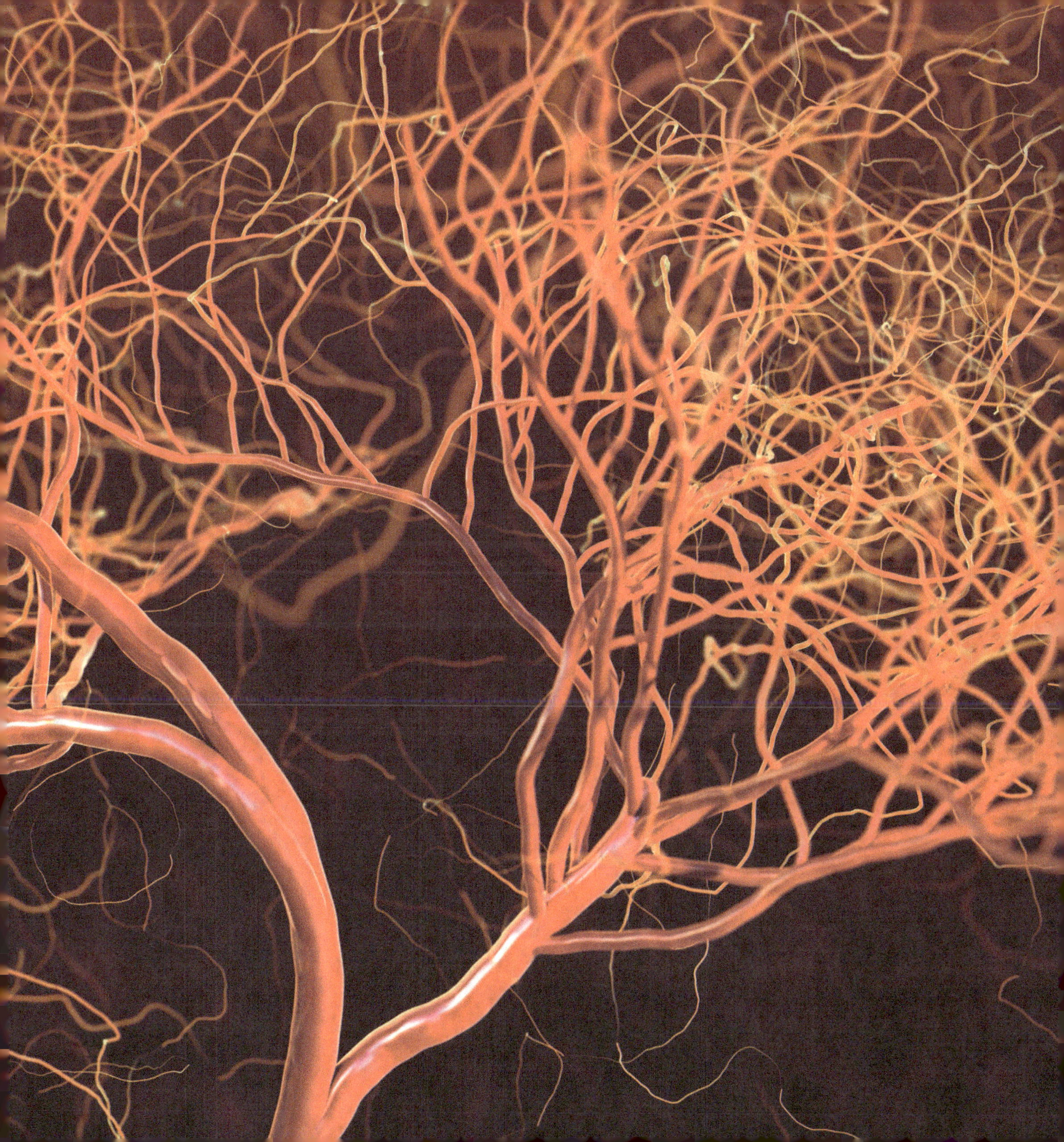

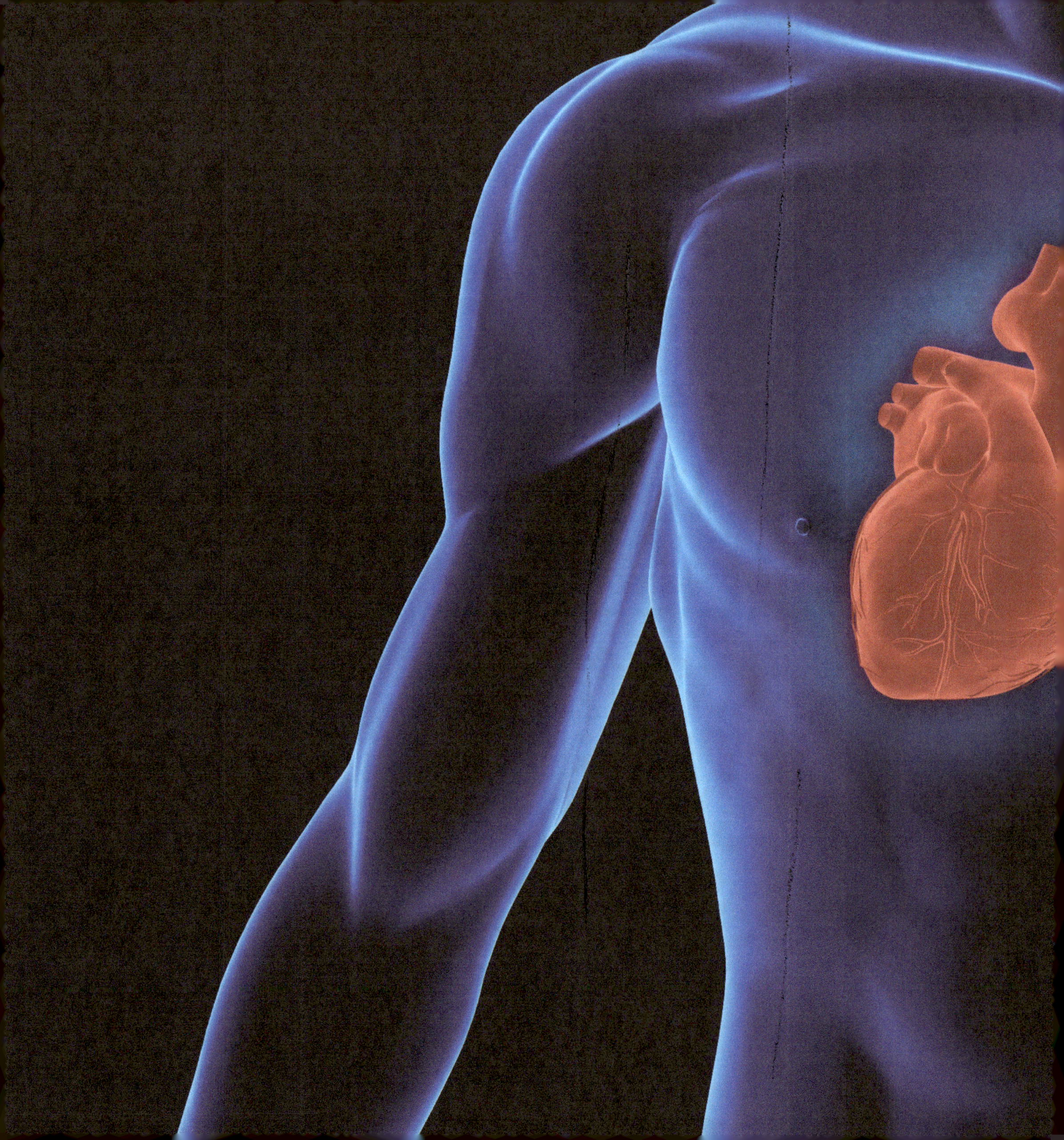

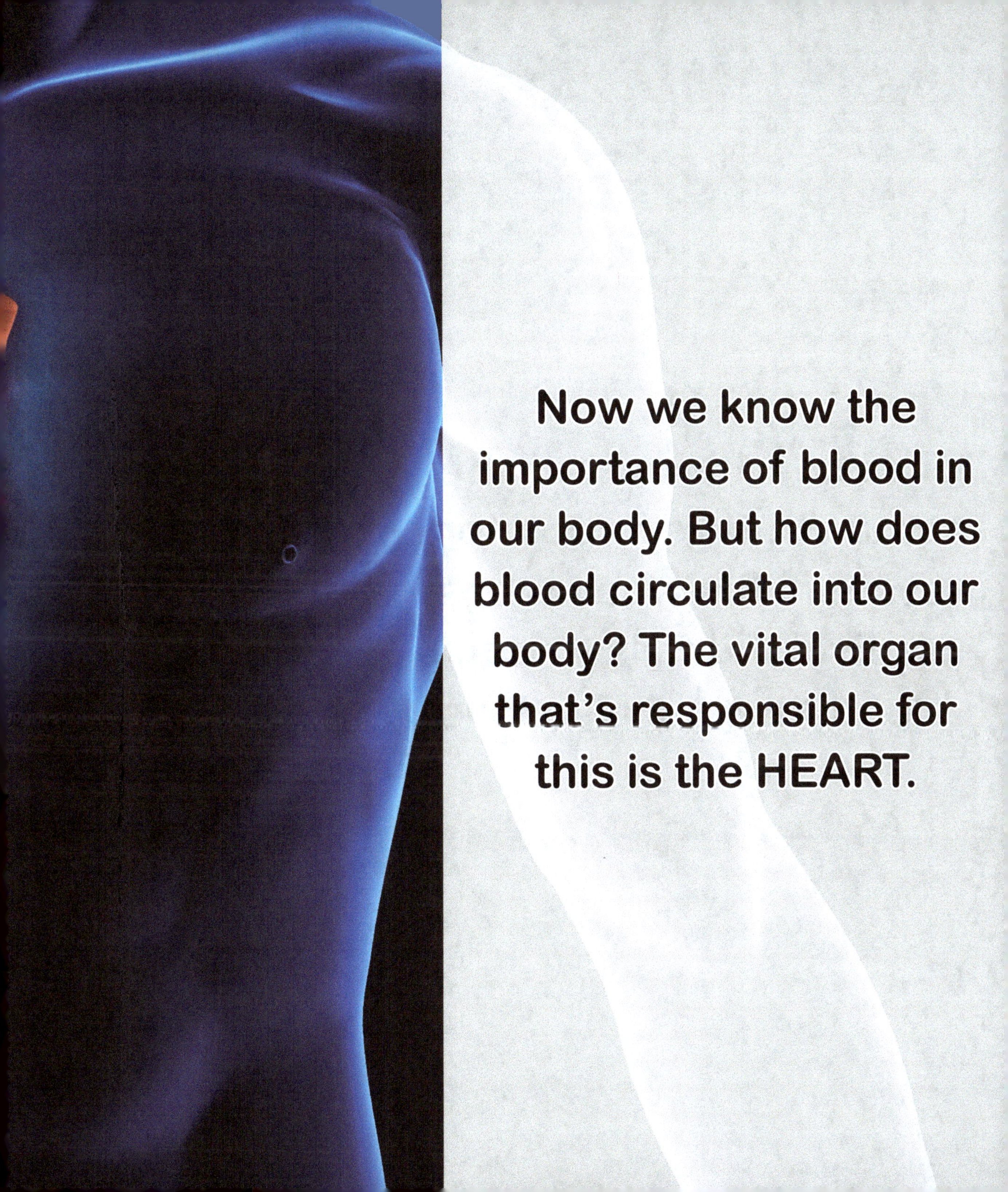
Now we know the importance of blood in our body. But how does blood circulate into our body? The vital organ that's responsible for this is the HEART.

The heart is part of the
human body's circulatory
system. It's what keeps
us alive. If it fails to pump
blood, then all else fails.

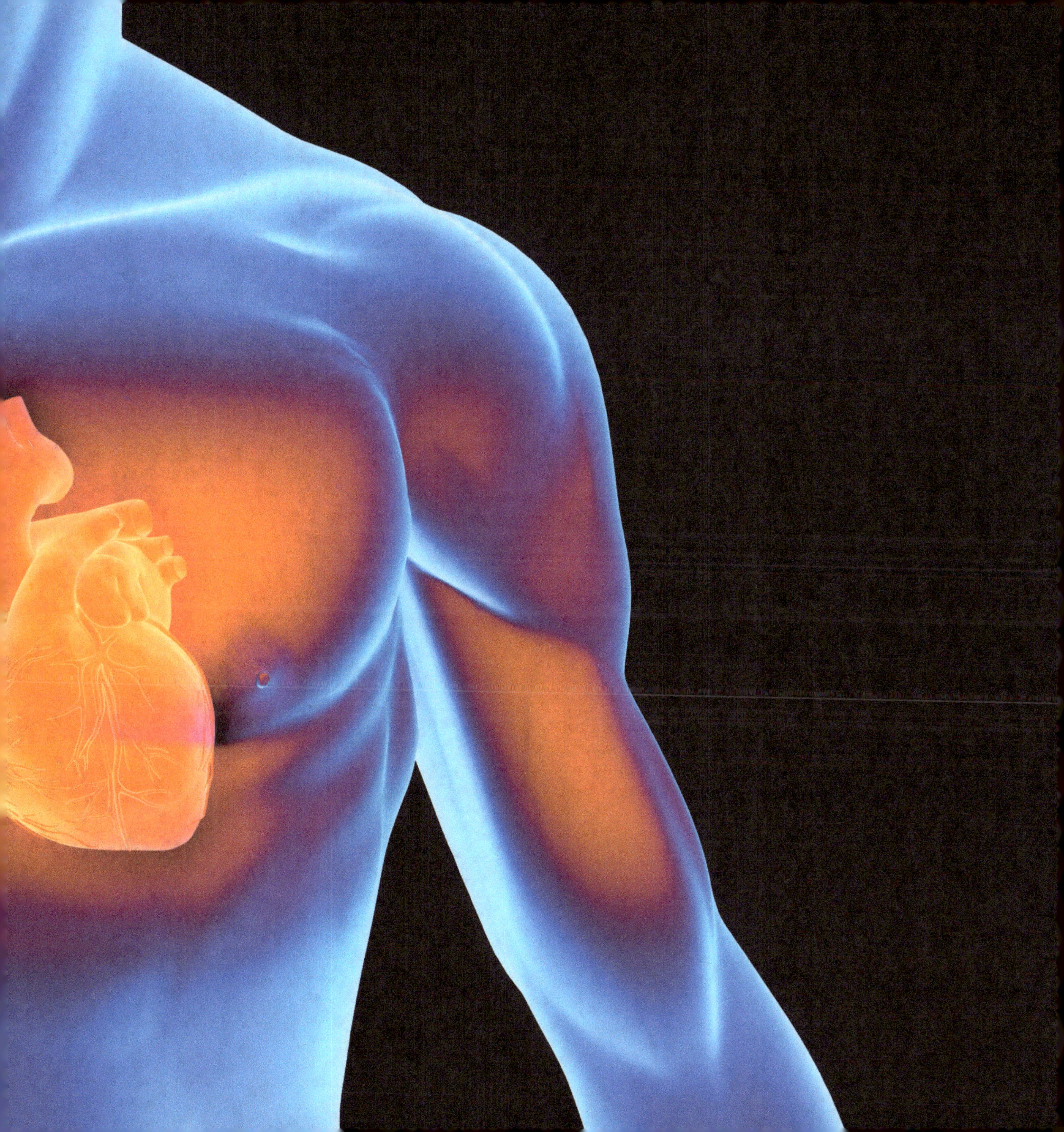

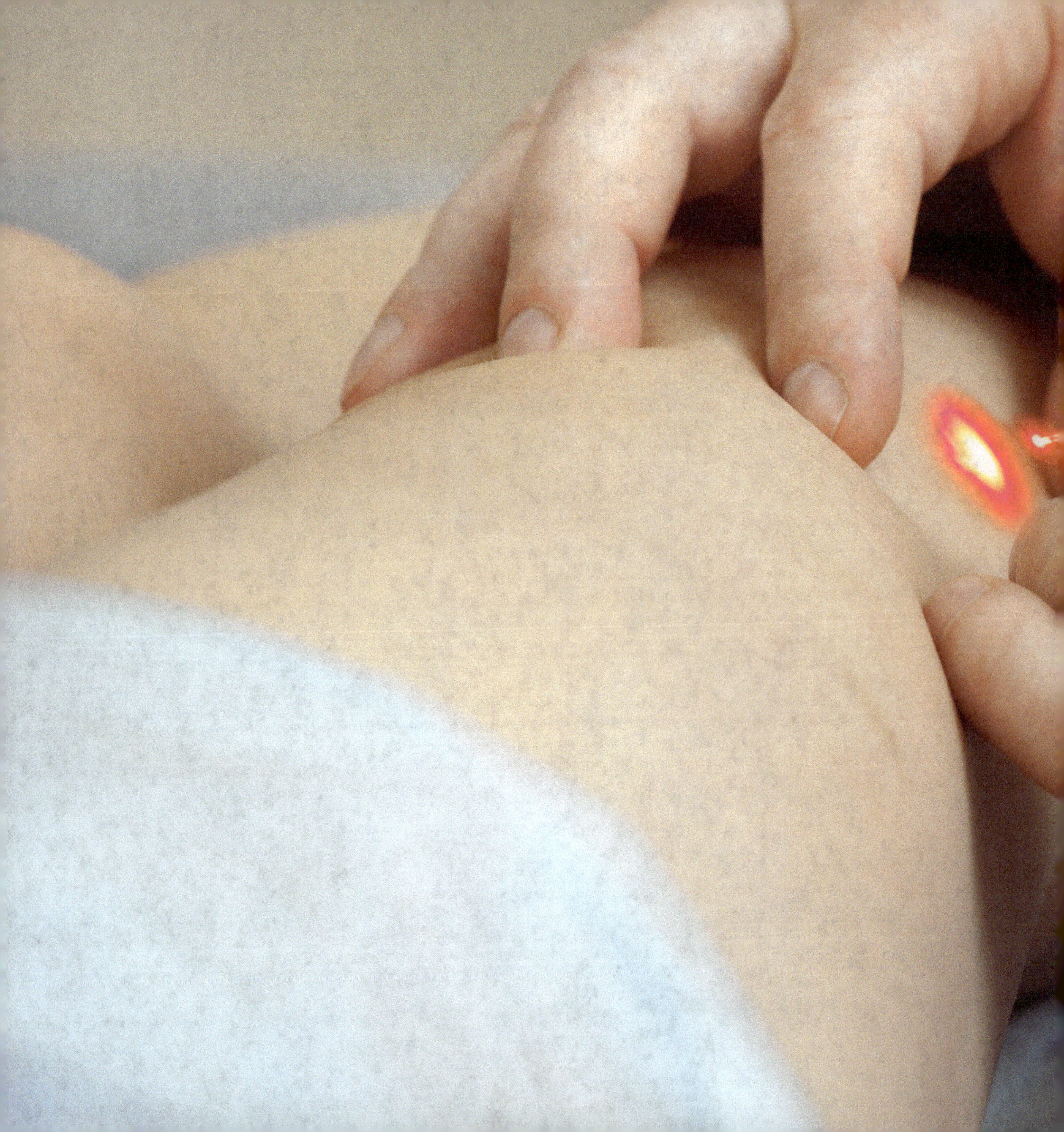

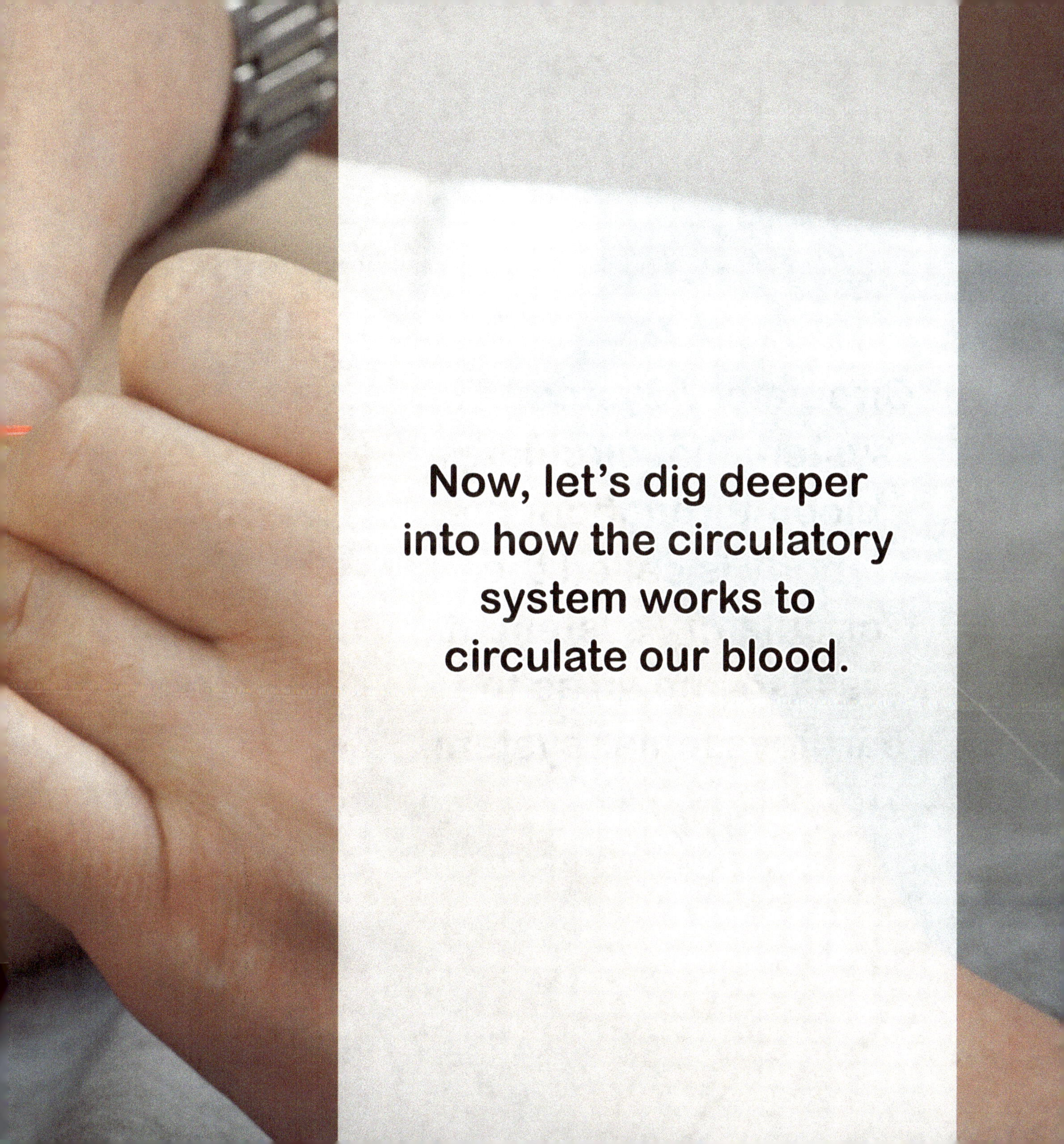

Now, let's dig deeper
into how the circulatory
system works to
circulate our blood.

Circulatory System. The system that circulates blood throughout the body is called the circulatory system. It is also known as the cardiovascular system.

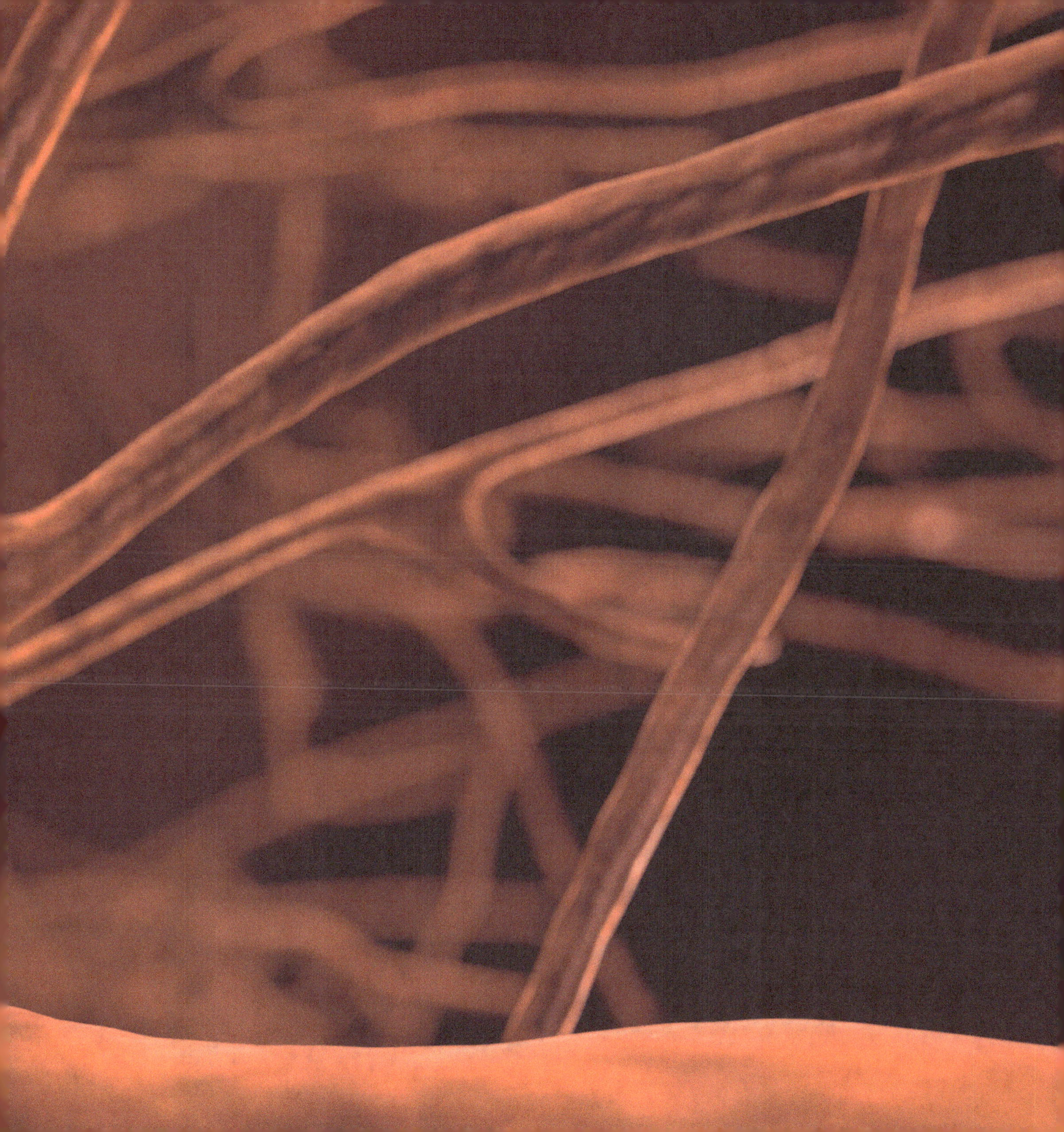

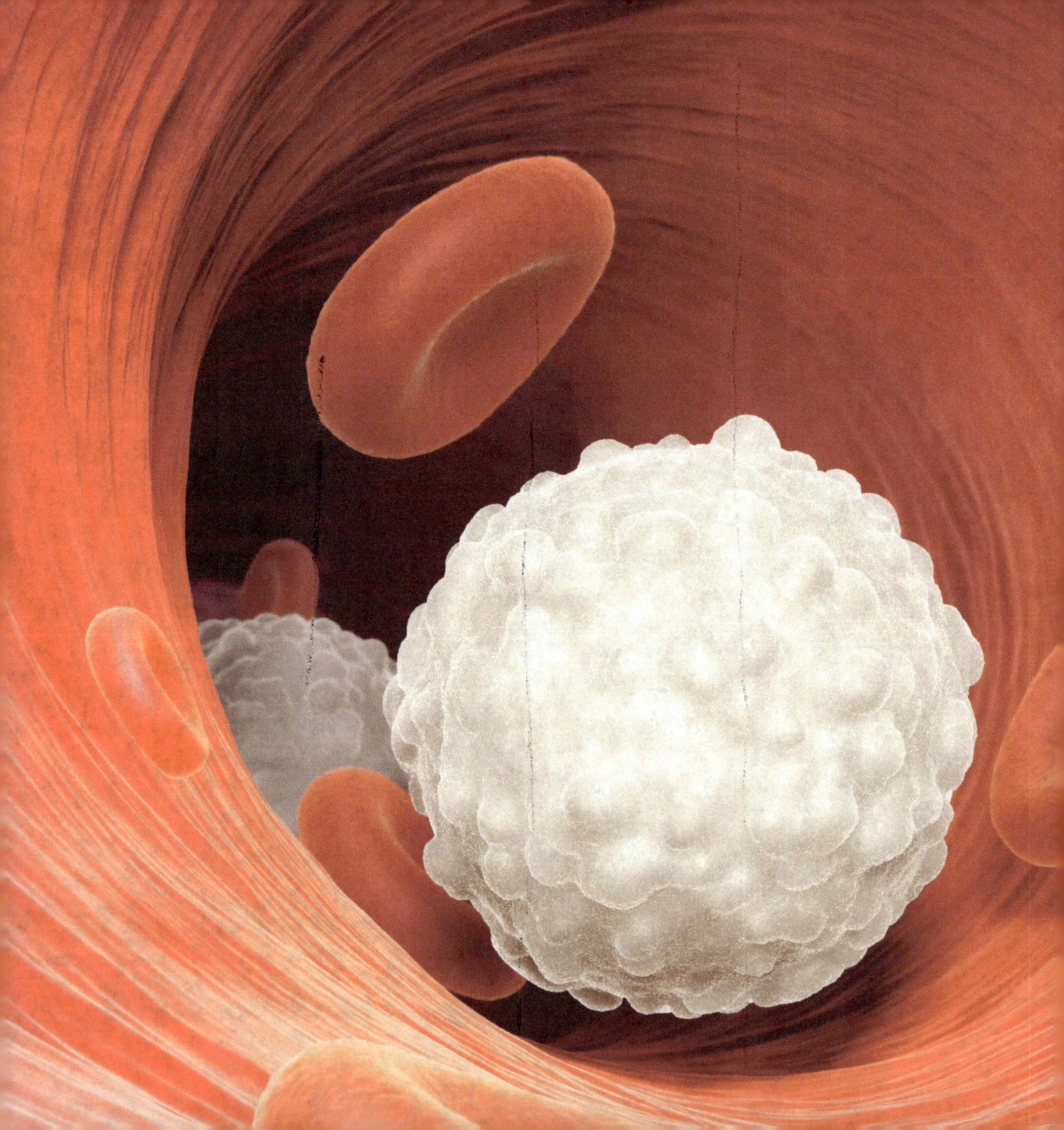

The essential parts of the system that work together are the heart, lungs, blood, and blood vessels. The blood vessels include the arteries, capillaries, and veins.

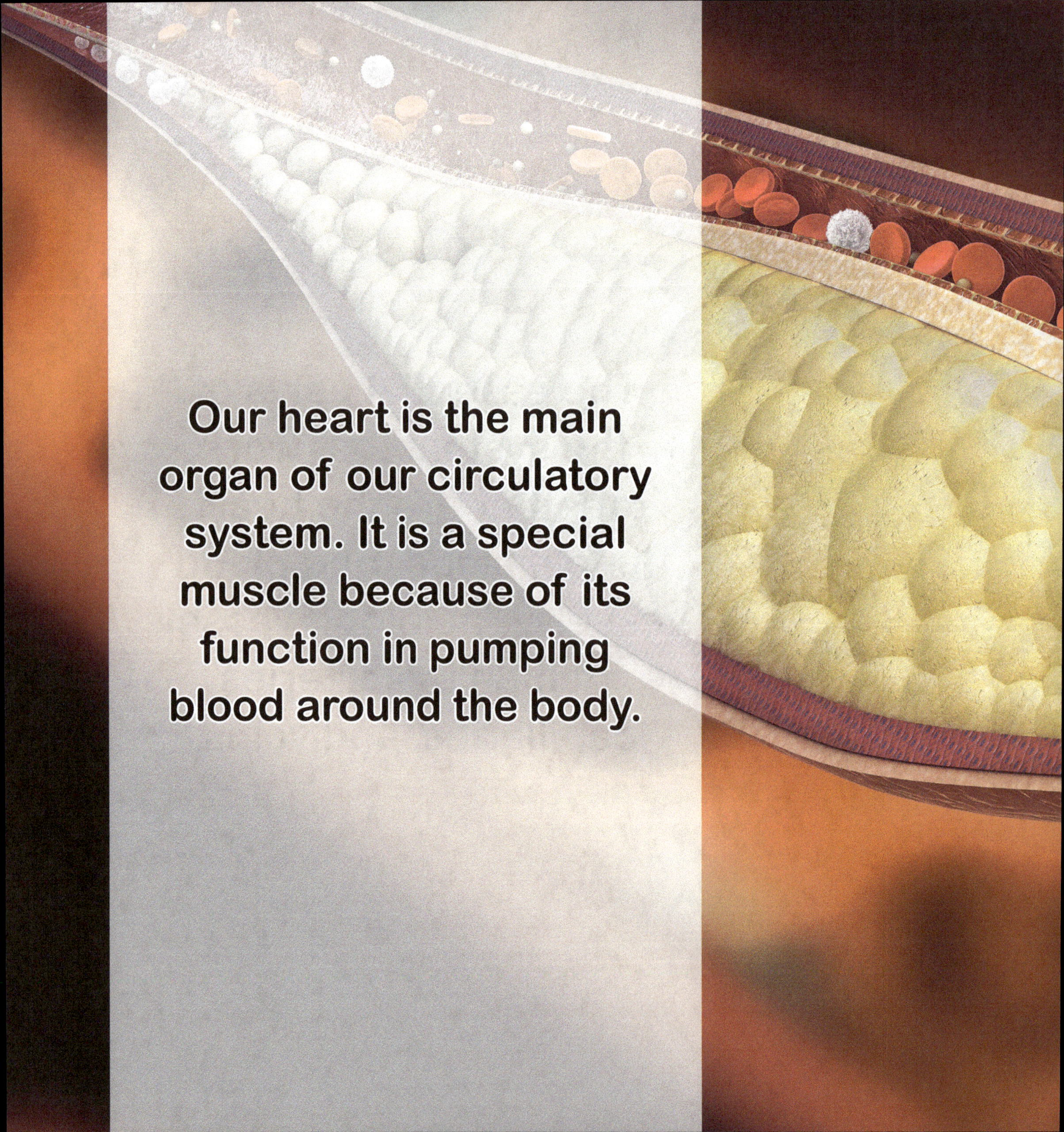

Our heart is the main
organ of our circulatory
system. It is a special
muscle because of its
function in pumping
blood around the body.

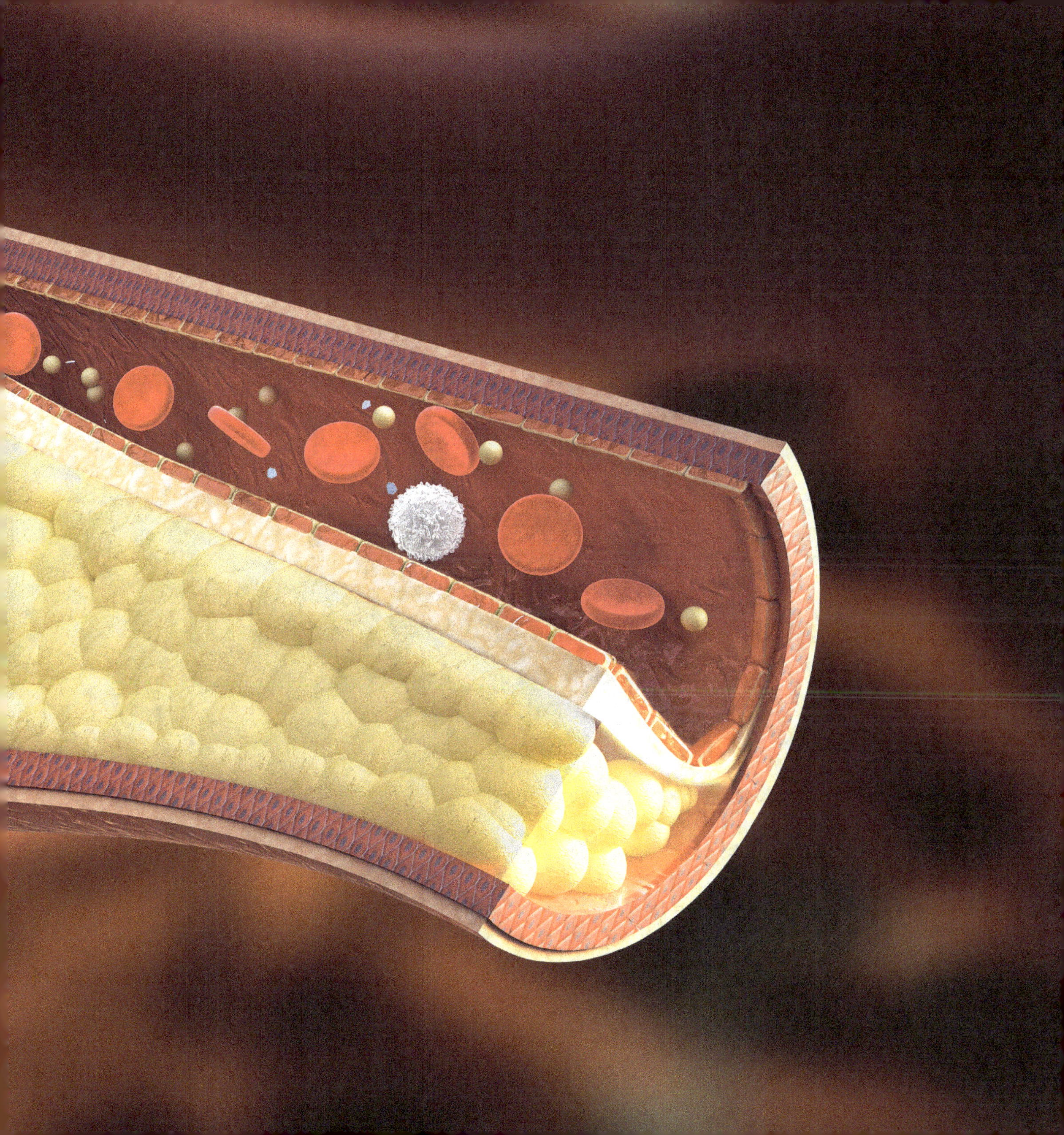

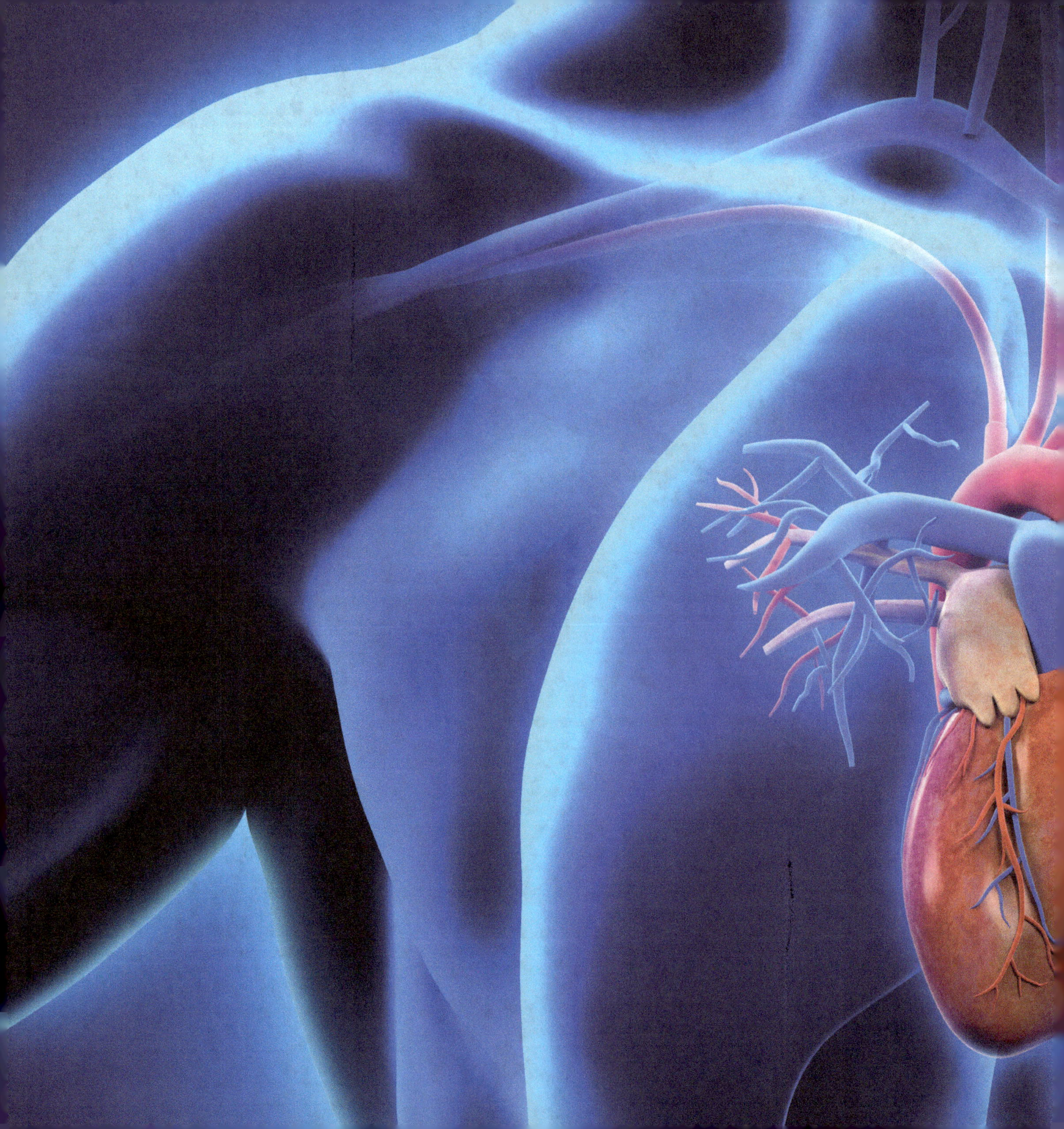

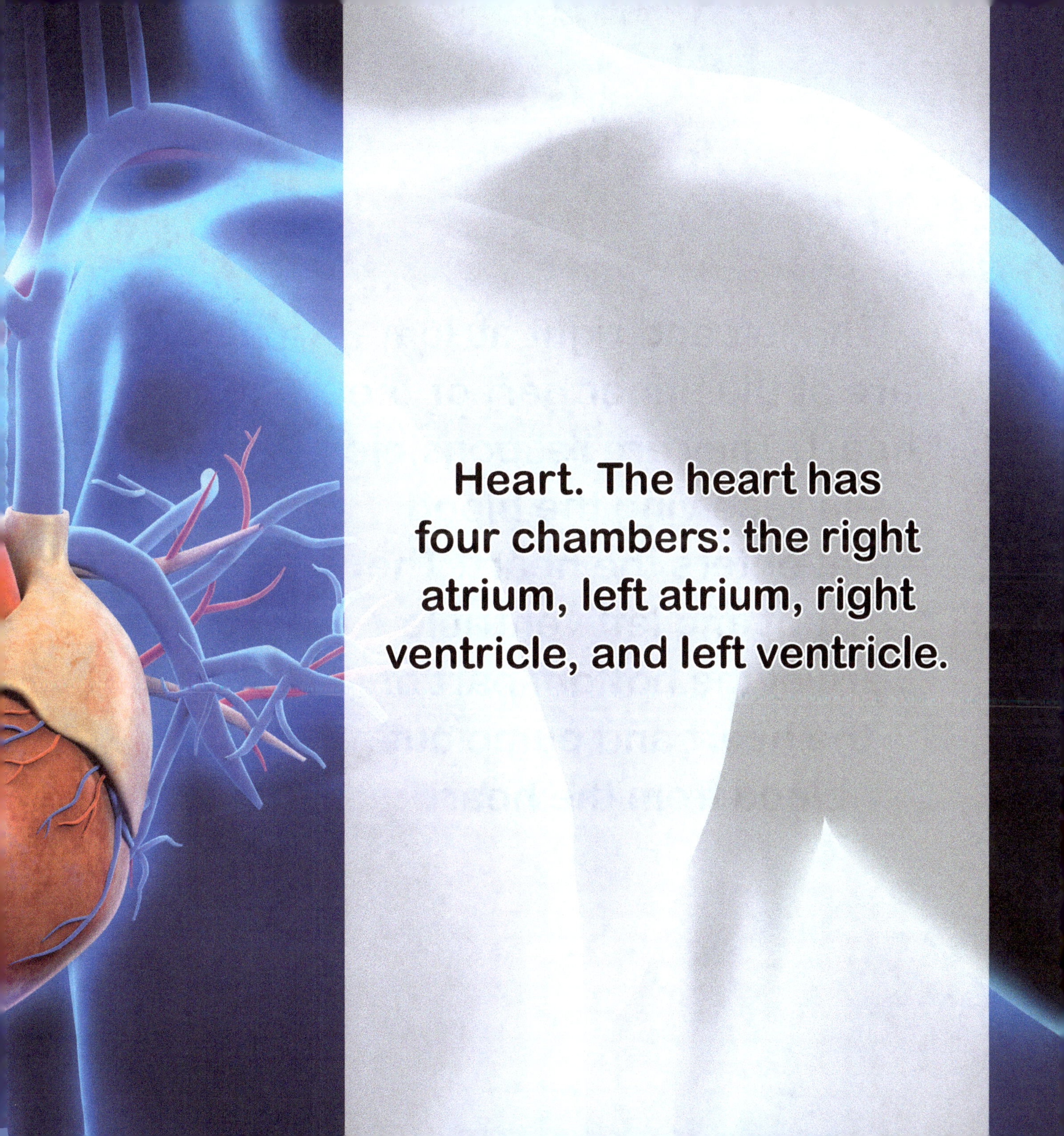

Heart. The heart has
four chambers: the right
atrium, left atrium, right
ventricle, and left ventricle.

The left and right atrium are at the upper part of the heart. They are responsible in receiving the blood that enters the heart. The right and left ventricle are at the bottom part of the heart and pump out blood from the heart.

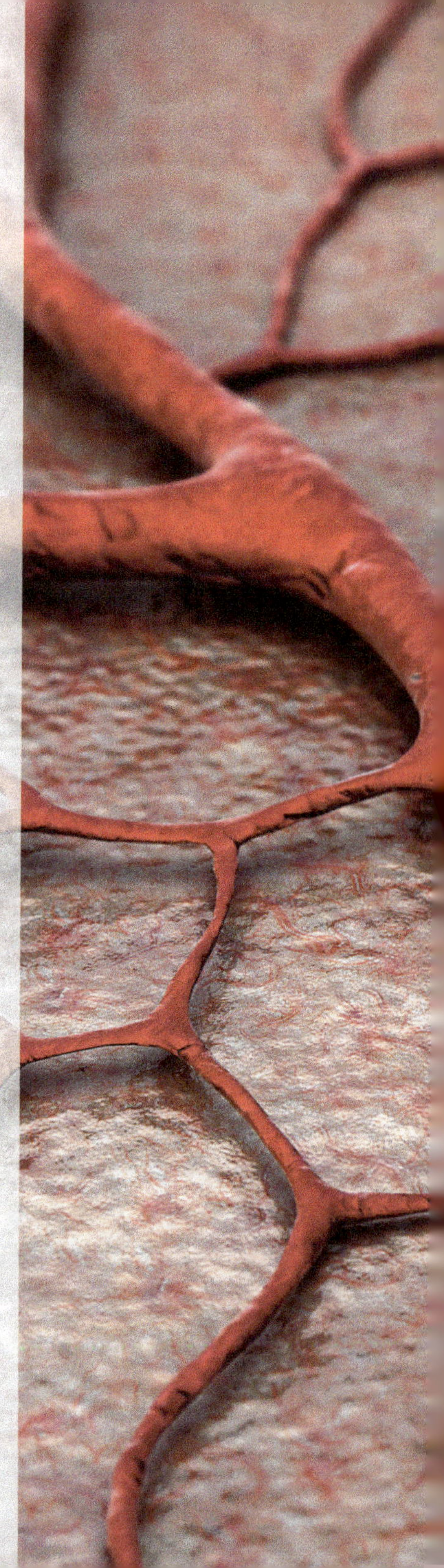

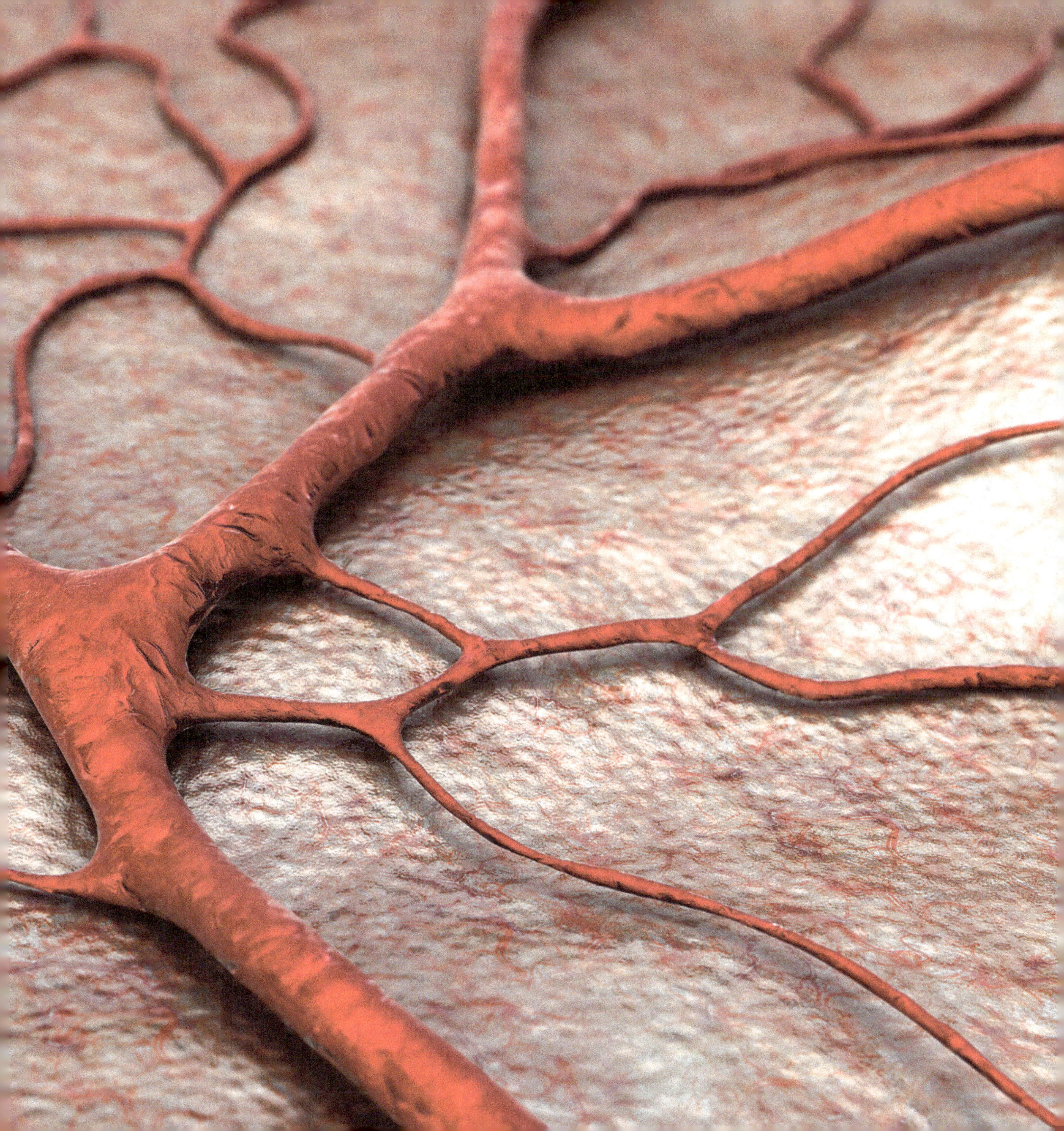

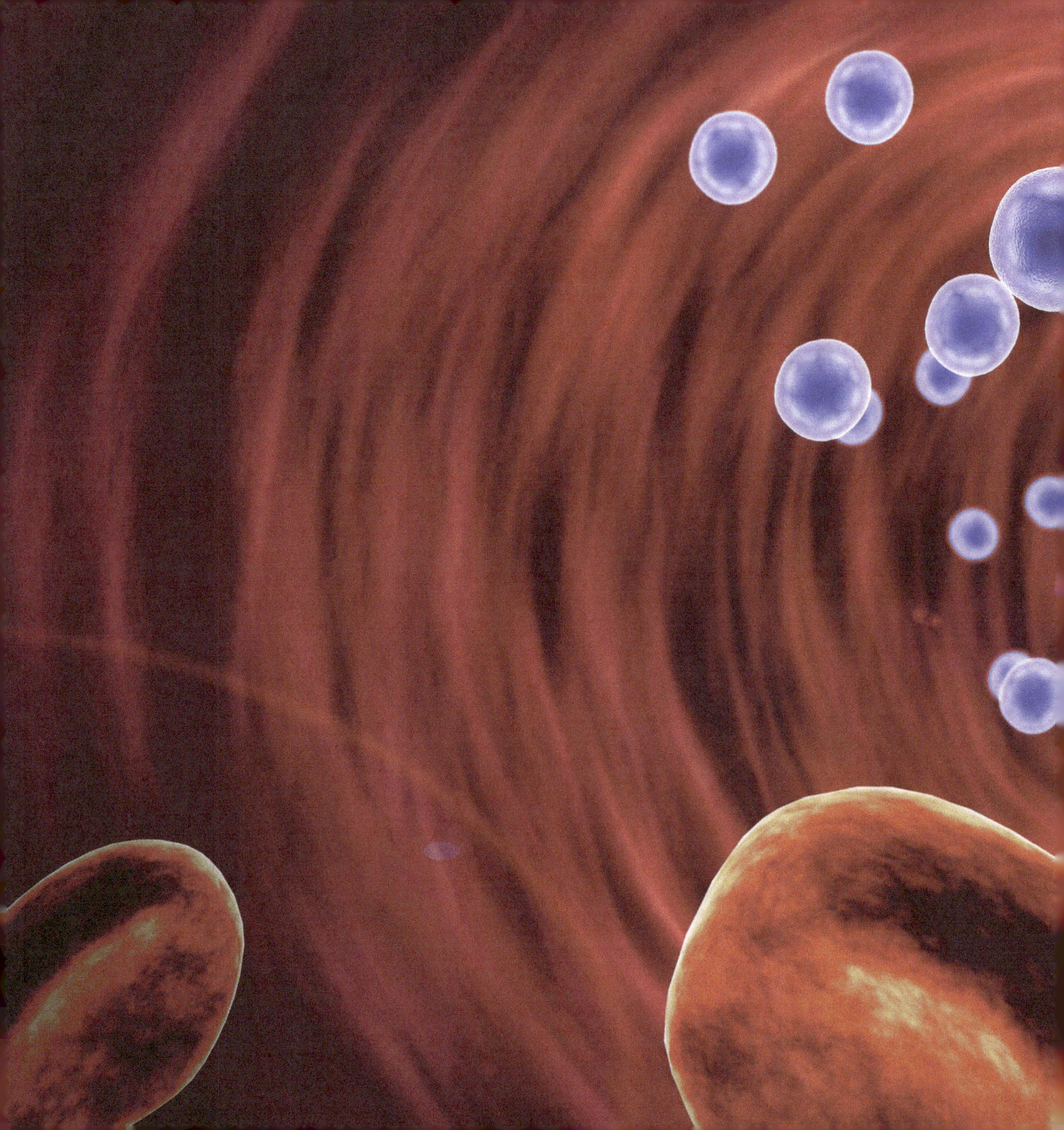

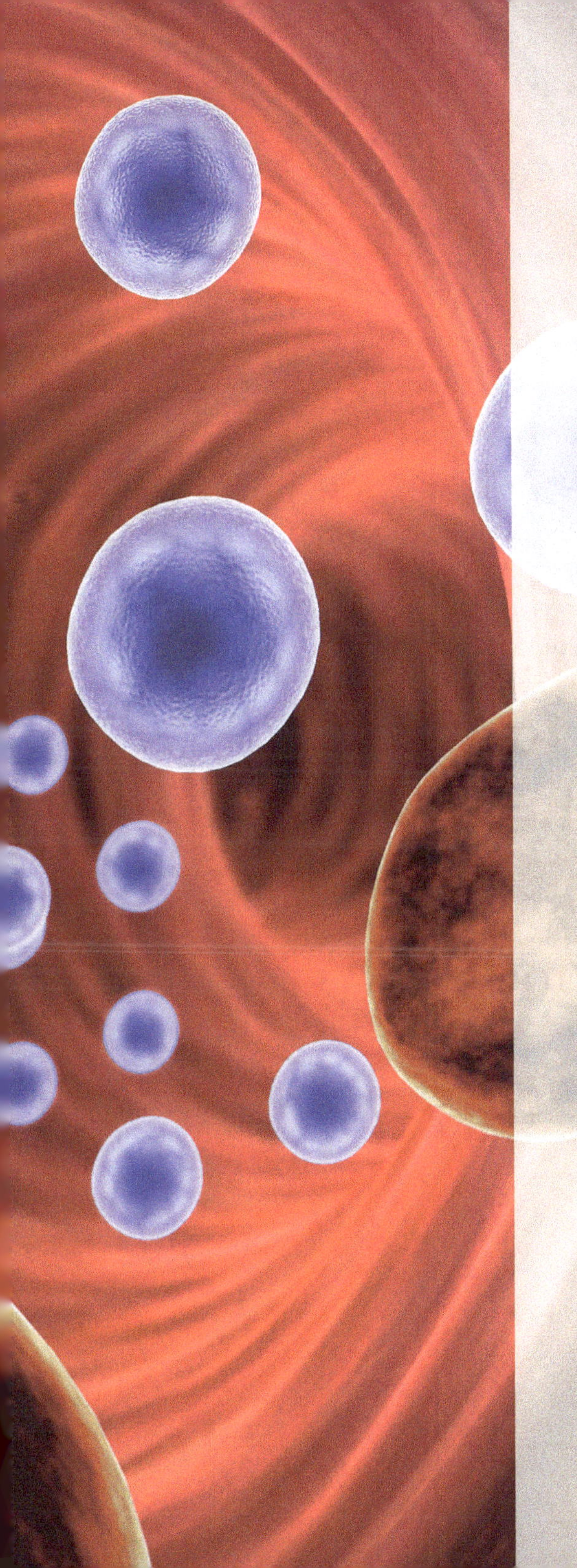

Here are the functions of each ventricle and atrium in the heart. The right atrium accepts deoxygenated blood and moves it to the right ventricle. And the right ventricle moves the deoxygenated blood to the lungs.

The left atrium accepts
oxygenated blood from
the lungs and moves it to
the left ventricle. And the
left ventricle moves the
oxygenated blood to the body.

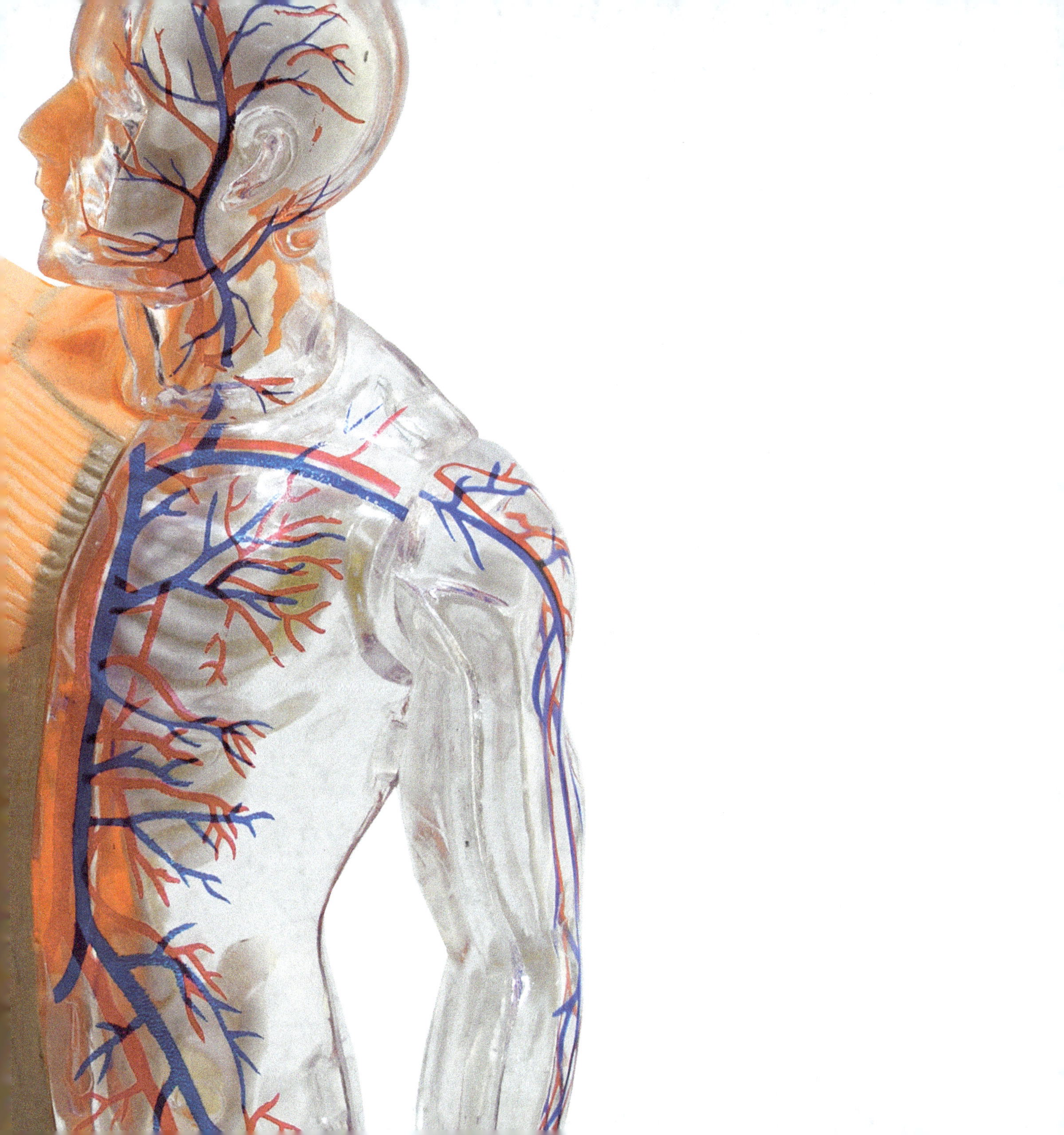

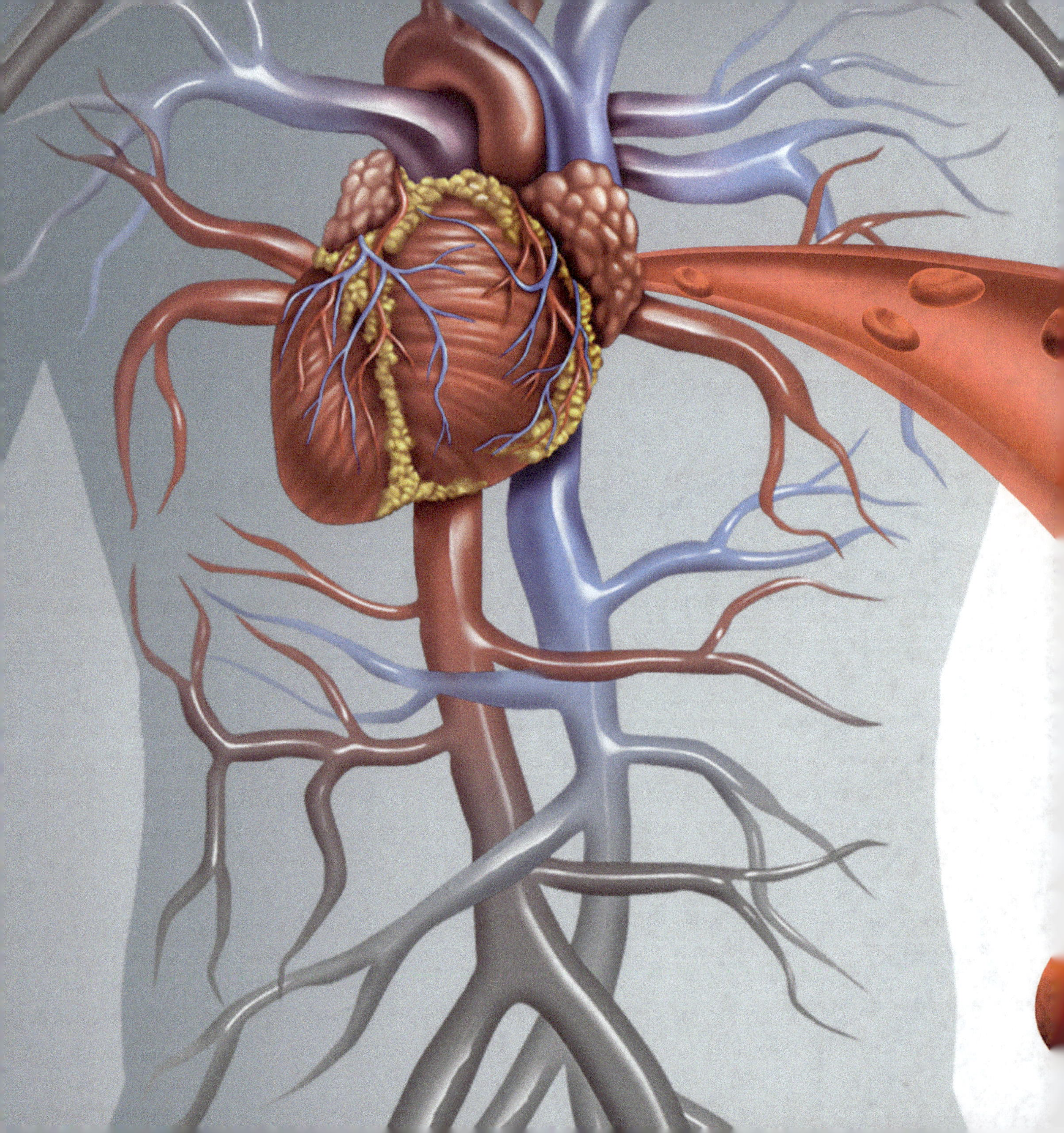

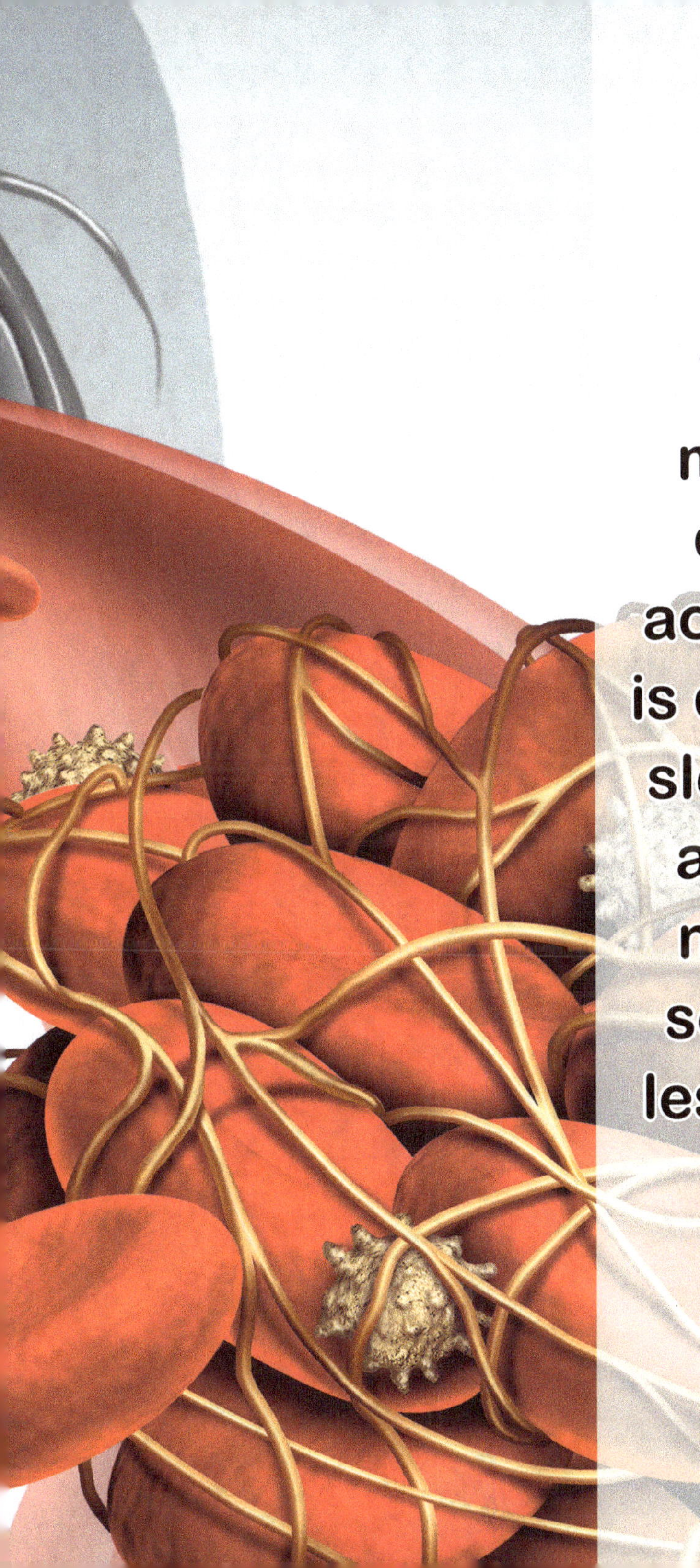

The heart pumps more or less blood depending on the activity that a person is doing. When we are sleeping, our body is at rest and doesn't need much oxygen so our heart pumps less blood than when we are active.

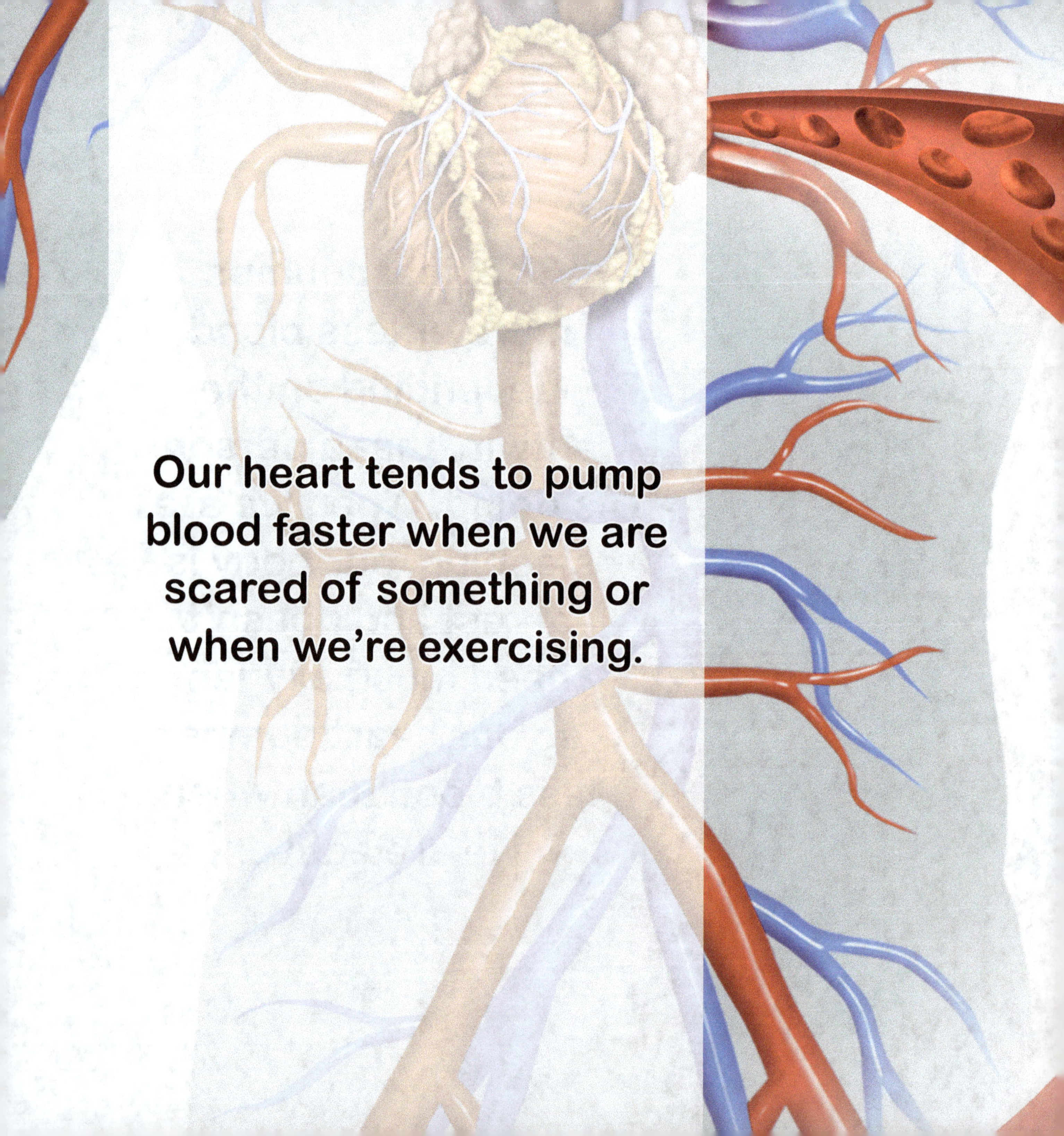
Our heart tends to pump
blood faster when we are
scared of something or
when we're exercising.

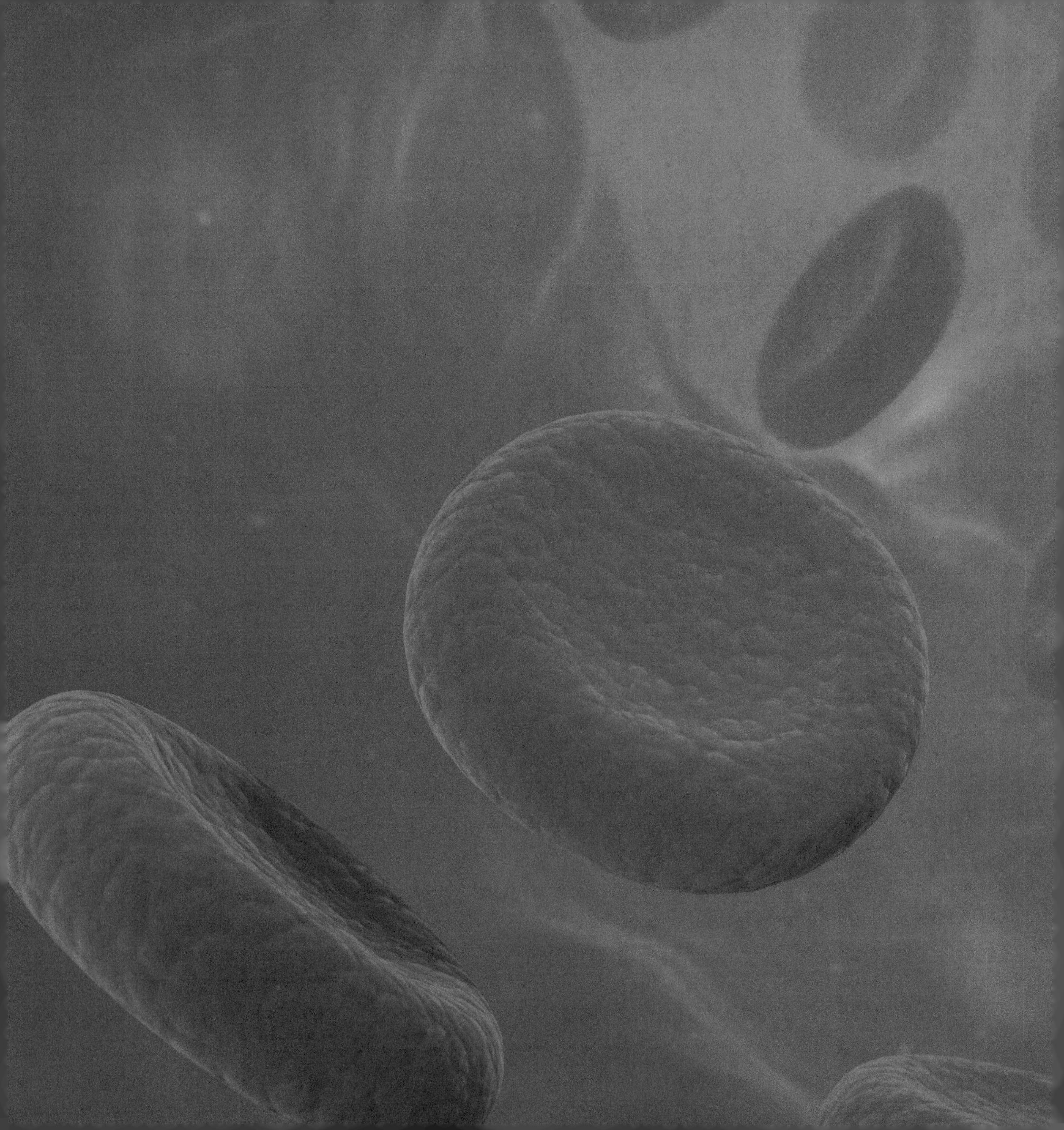

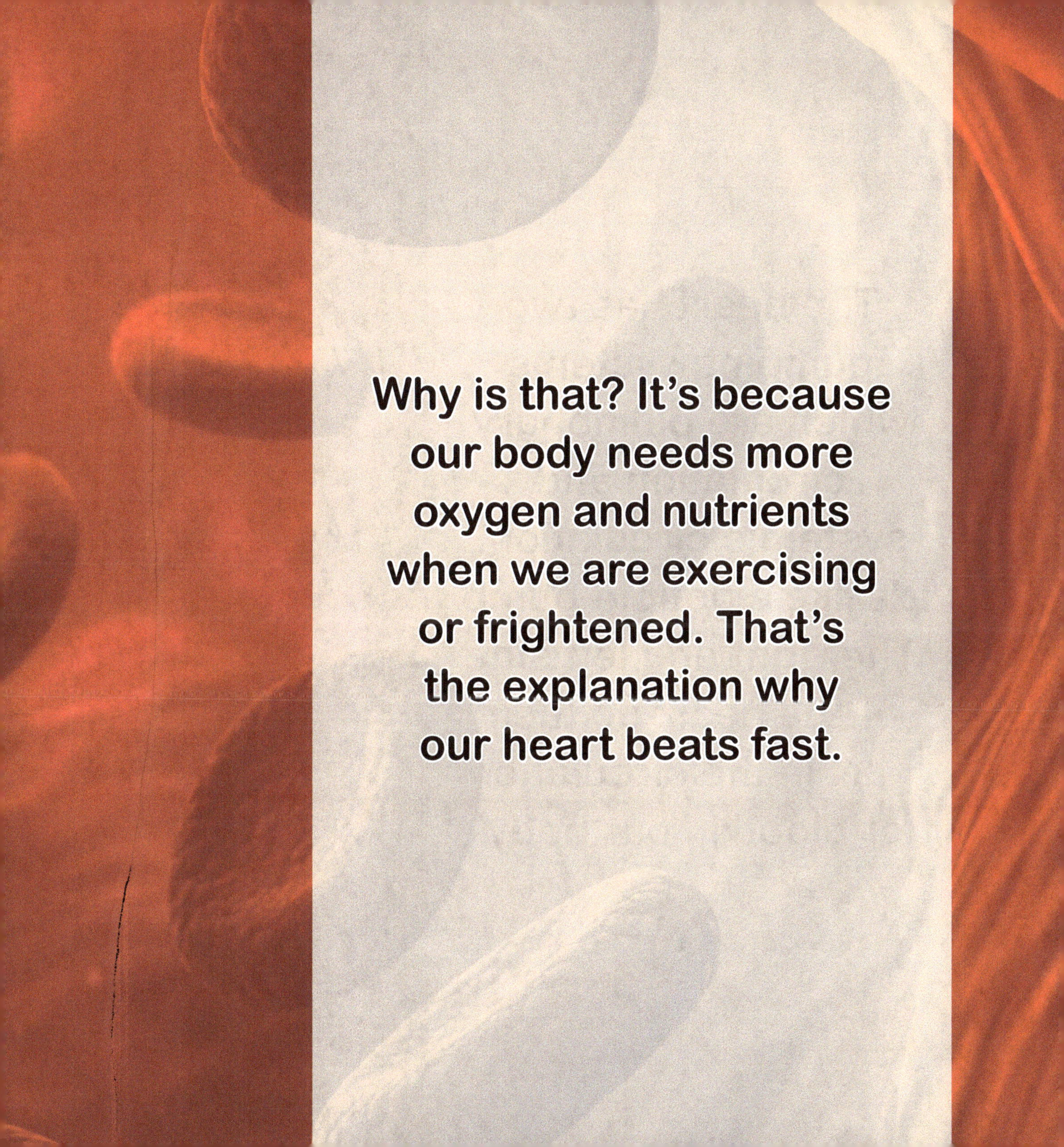

Why is that? It's because our body needs more oxygen and nutrients when we are exercising or frightened. That's the explanation why our heart beats fast.

The heart has two
pumping systems
which are pulmonary
circulation and
systemic circulation.
It's like a double-pump.
The right and left side
of the heart do their
part in the circulation
of blood in our body.

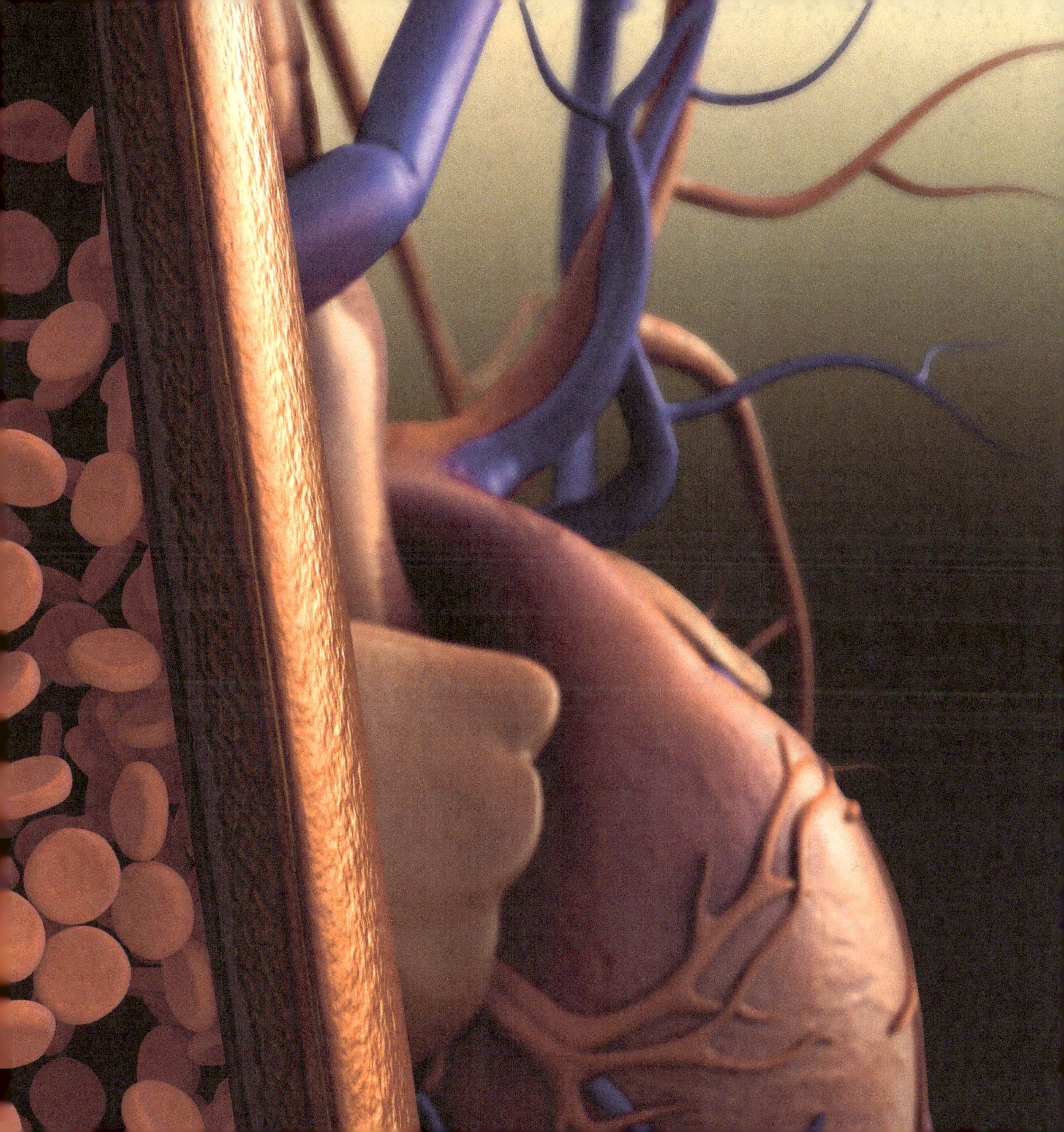

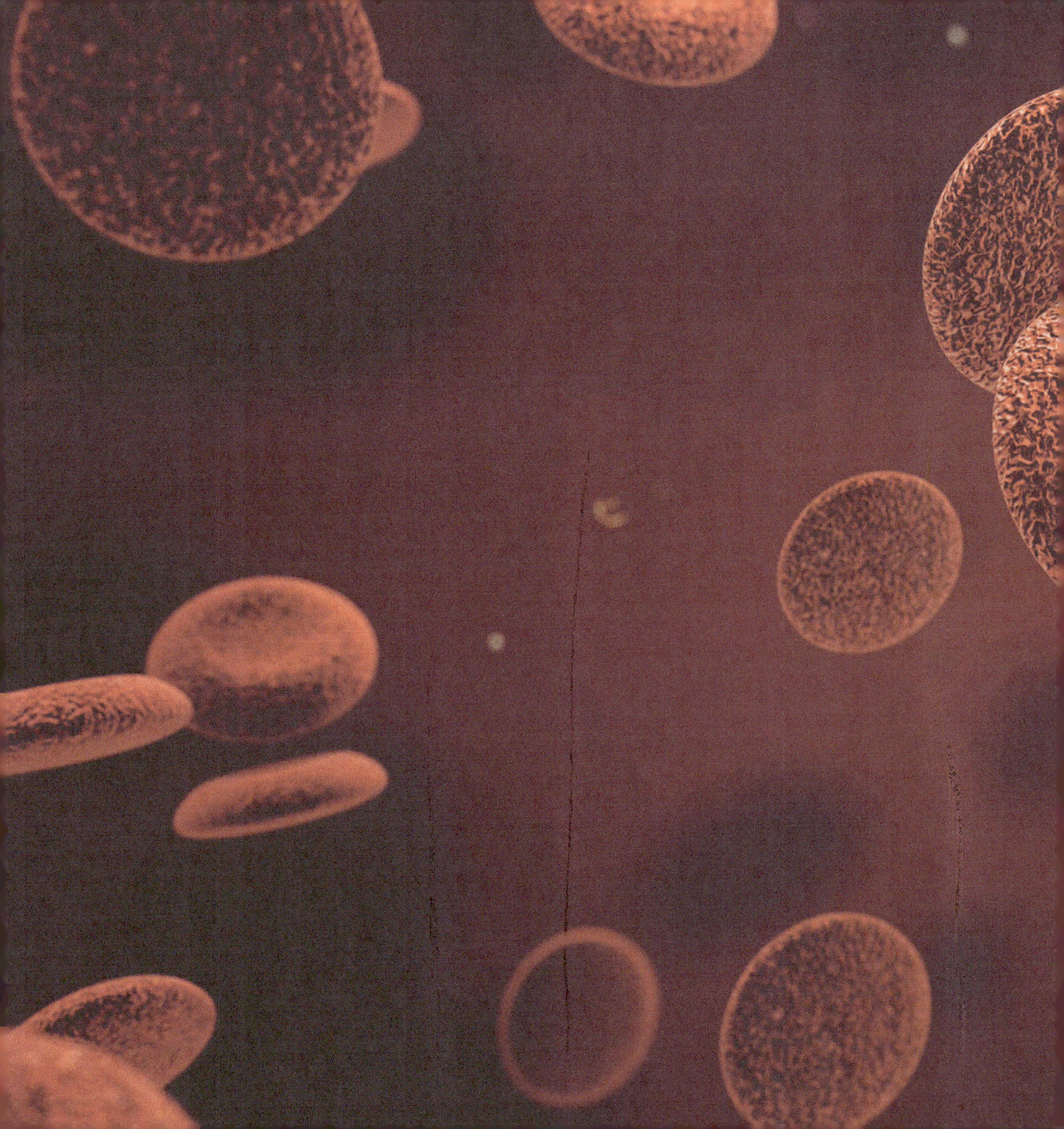

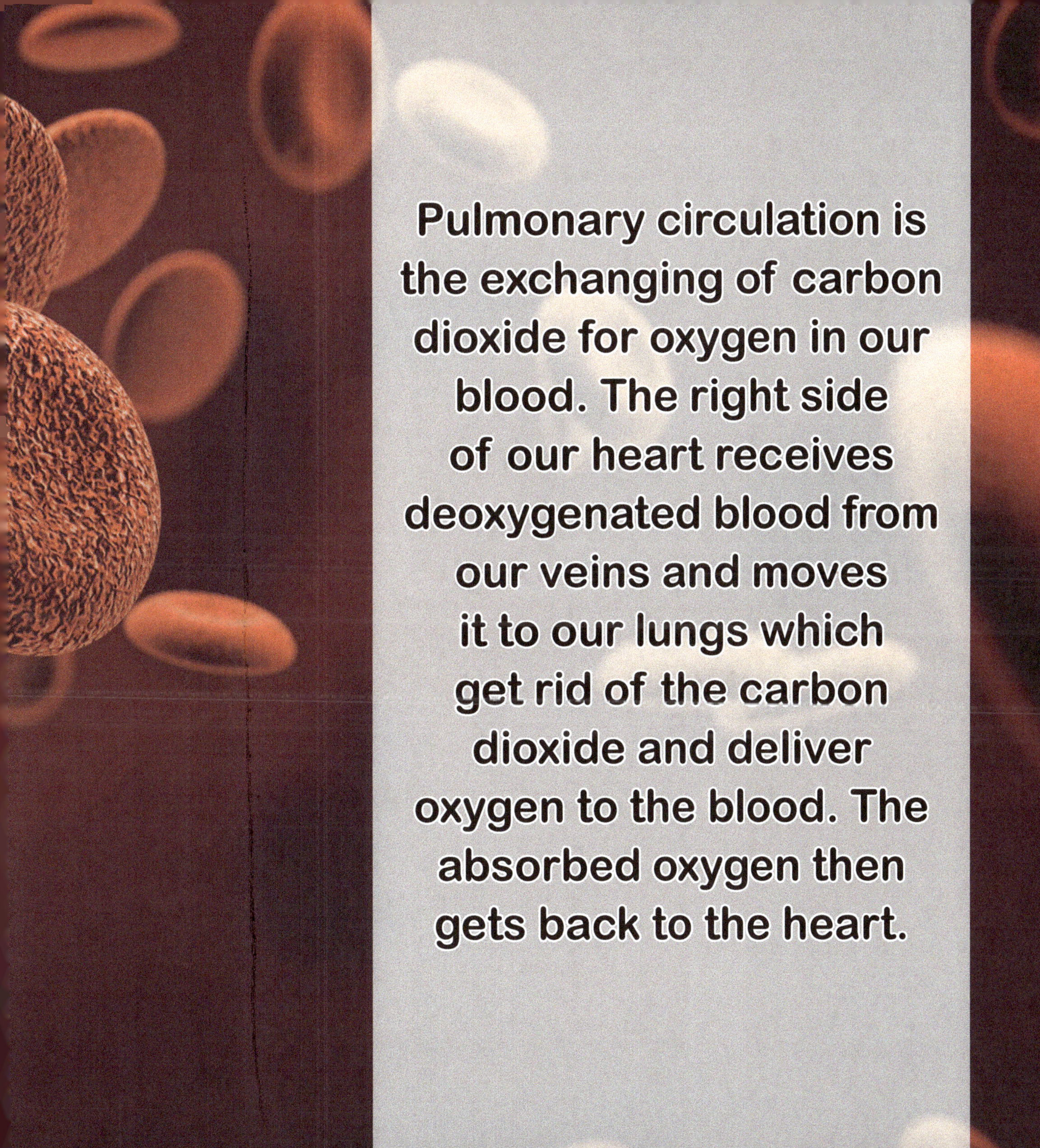

Pulmonary circulation is
the exchanging of carbon
dioxide for oxygen in our
blood. The right side
of our heart receives
deoxygenated blood from
our veins and moves
it to our lungs which
get rid of the carbon
dioxide and deliver
oxygen to the blood. The
absorbed oxygen then
gets back to the heart.

Systemic circulation is the movement of blood from the heart through the rest of the body and back to the heart.

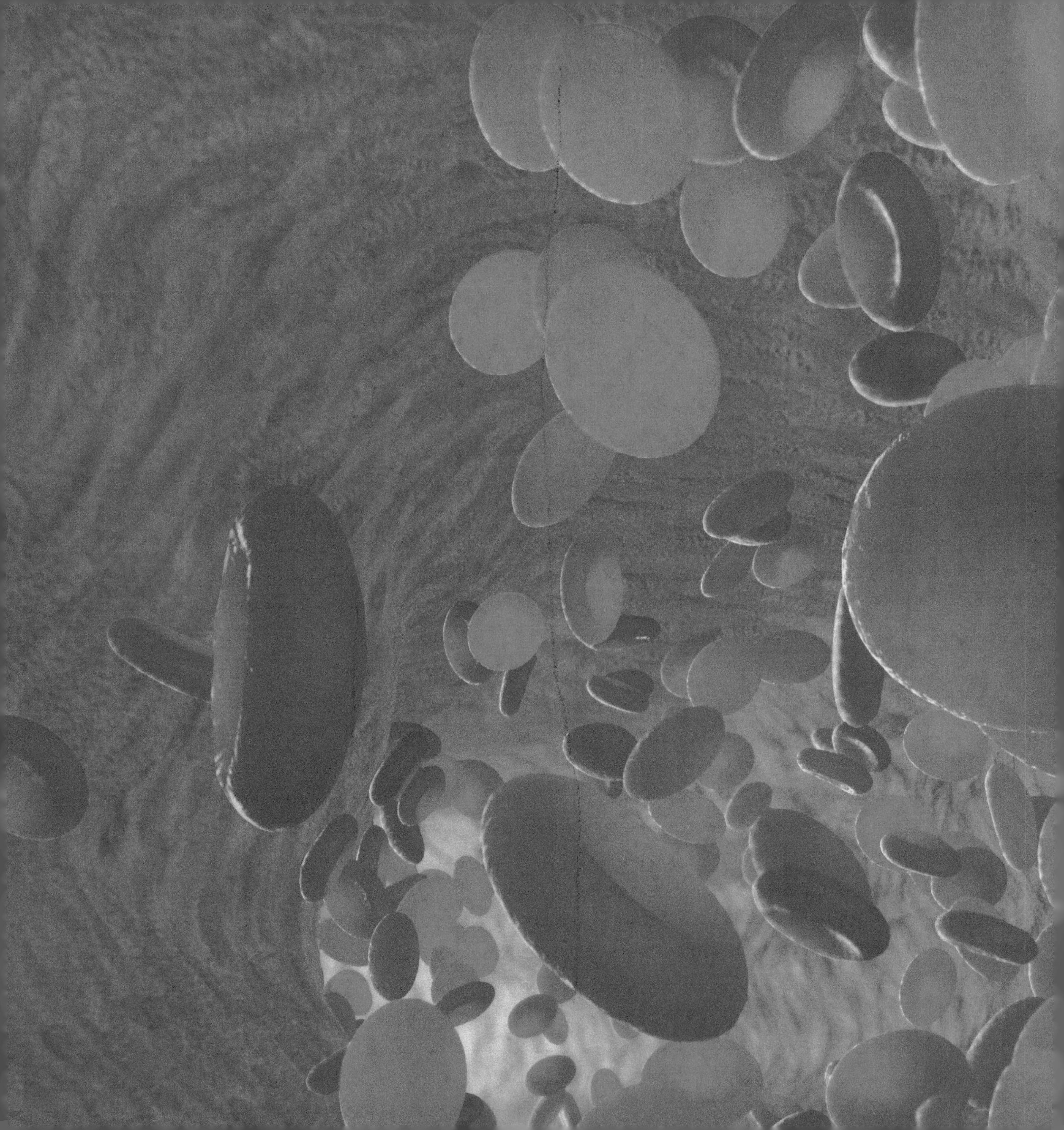

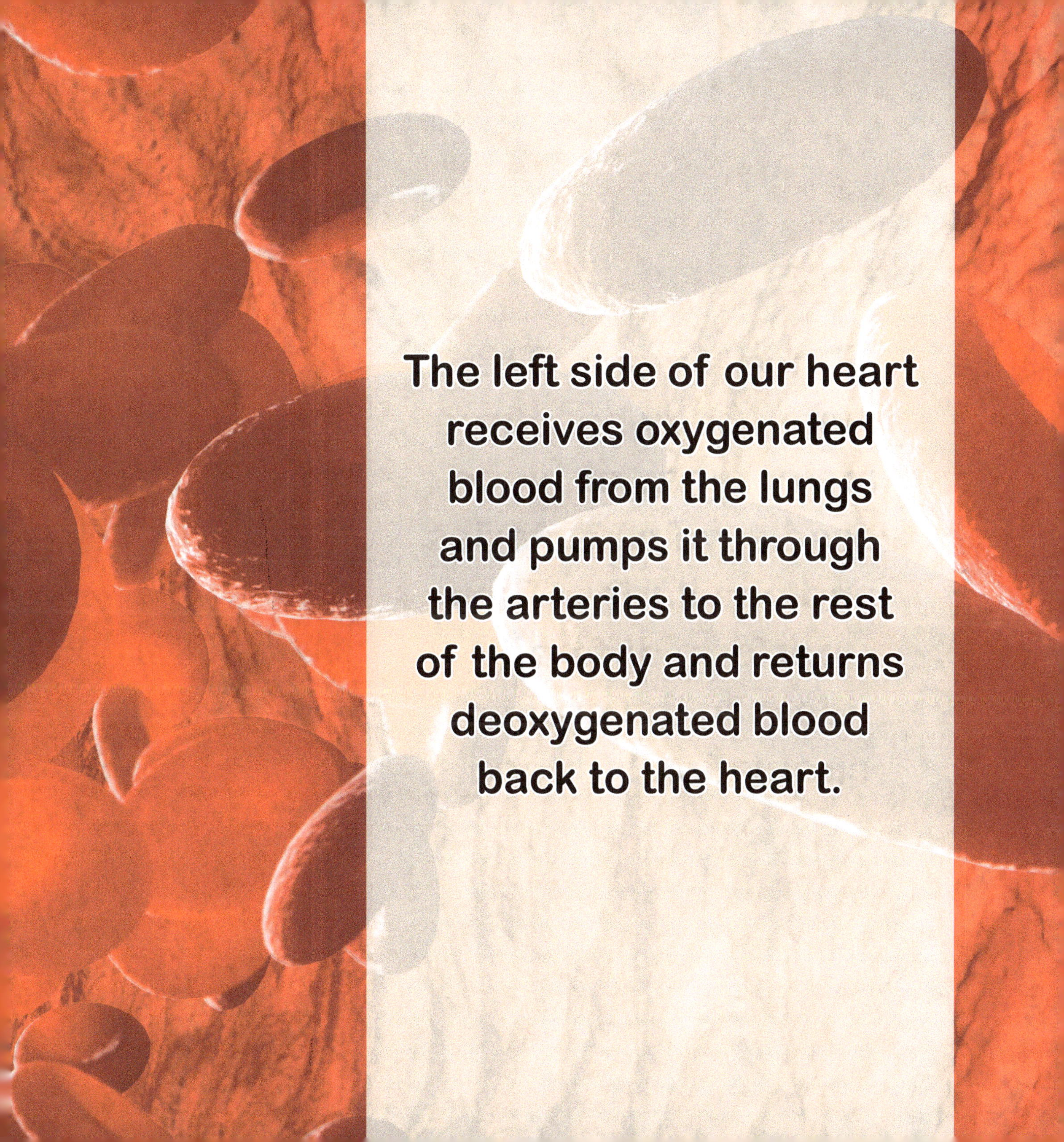

The left side of our heart receives oxygenated blood from the lungs and pumps it through the arteries to the rest of the body and returns deoxygenated blood back to the heart.

Blood Vessels. The human body has three major types of blood vessels: veins, arteries and capillaries. They perform different tasks in the proper circulation of blood.

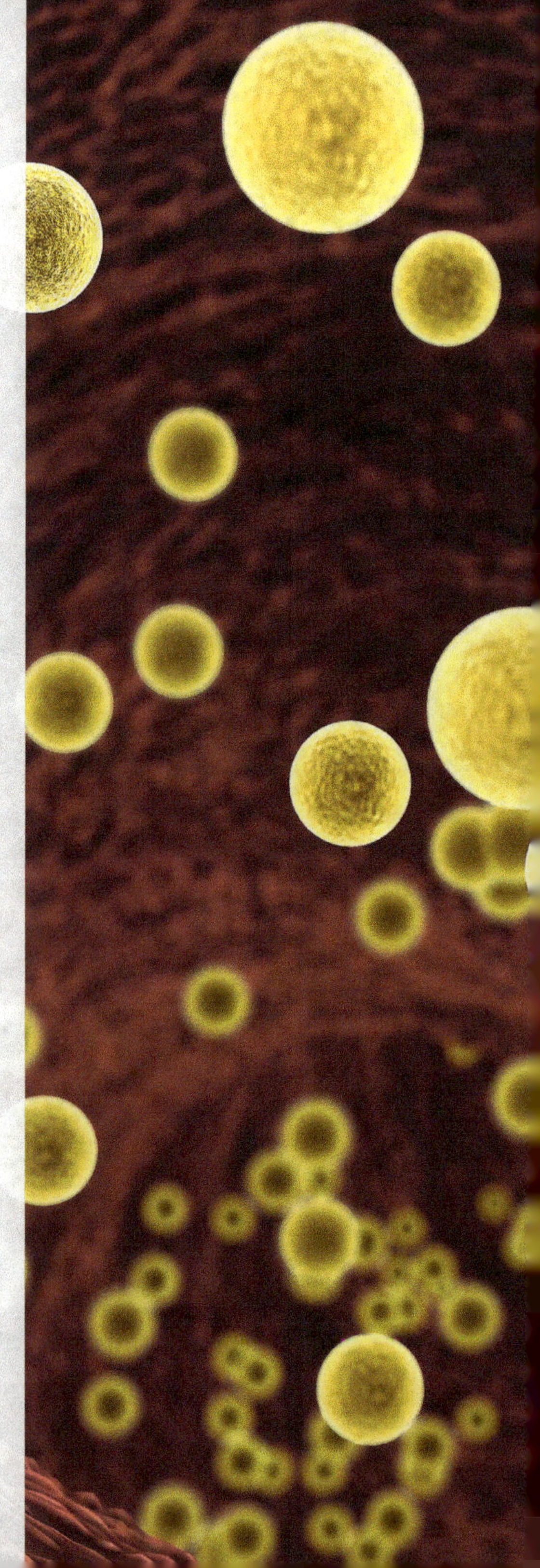

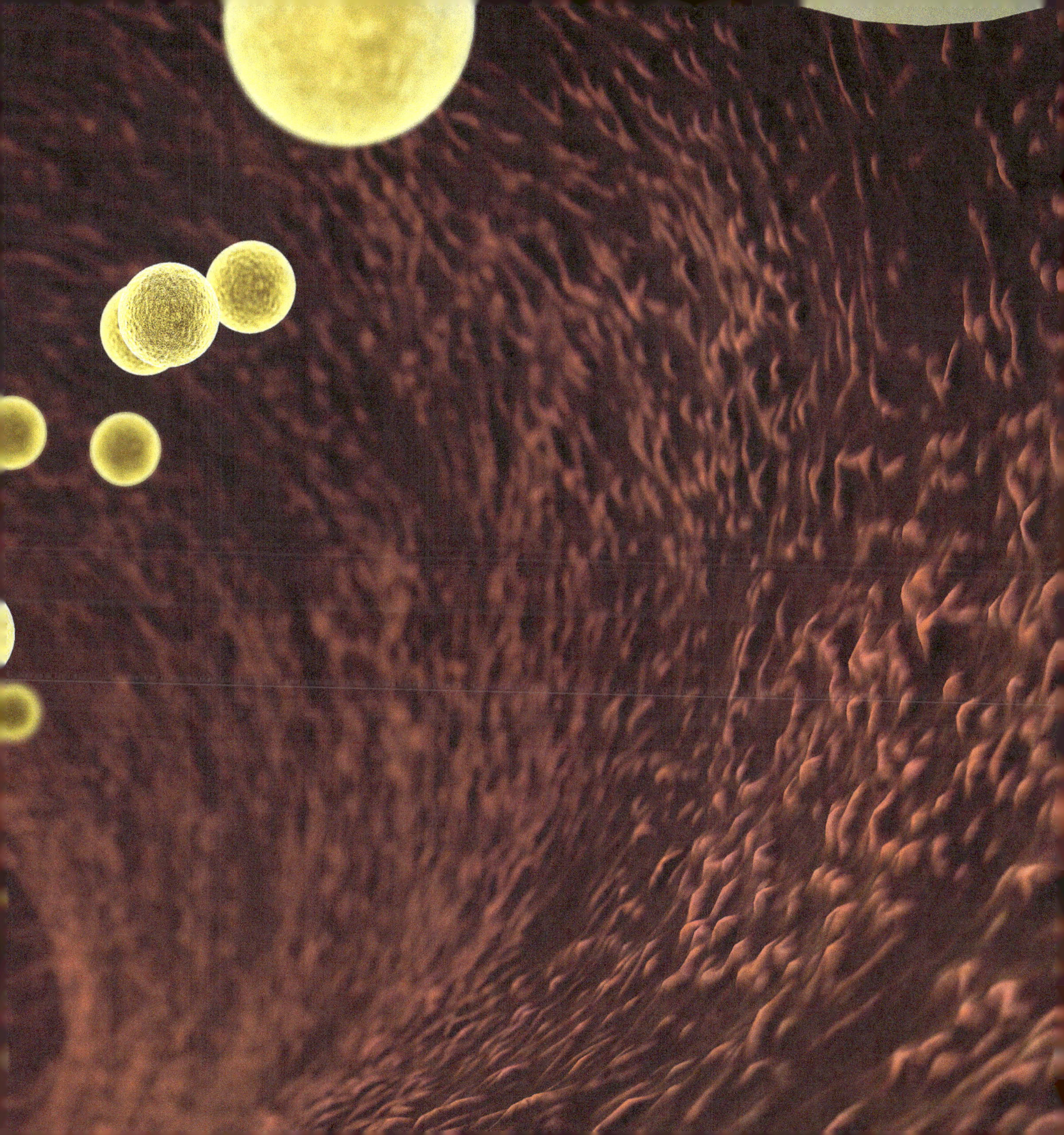

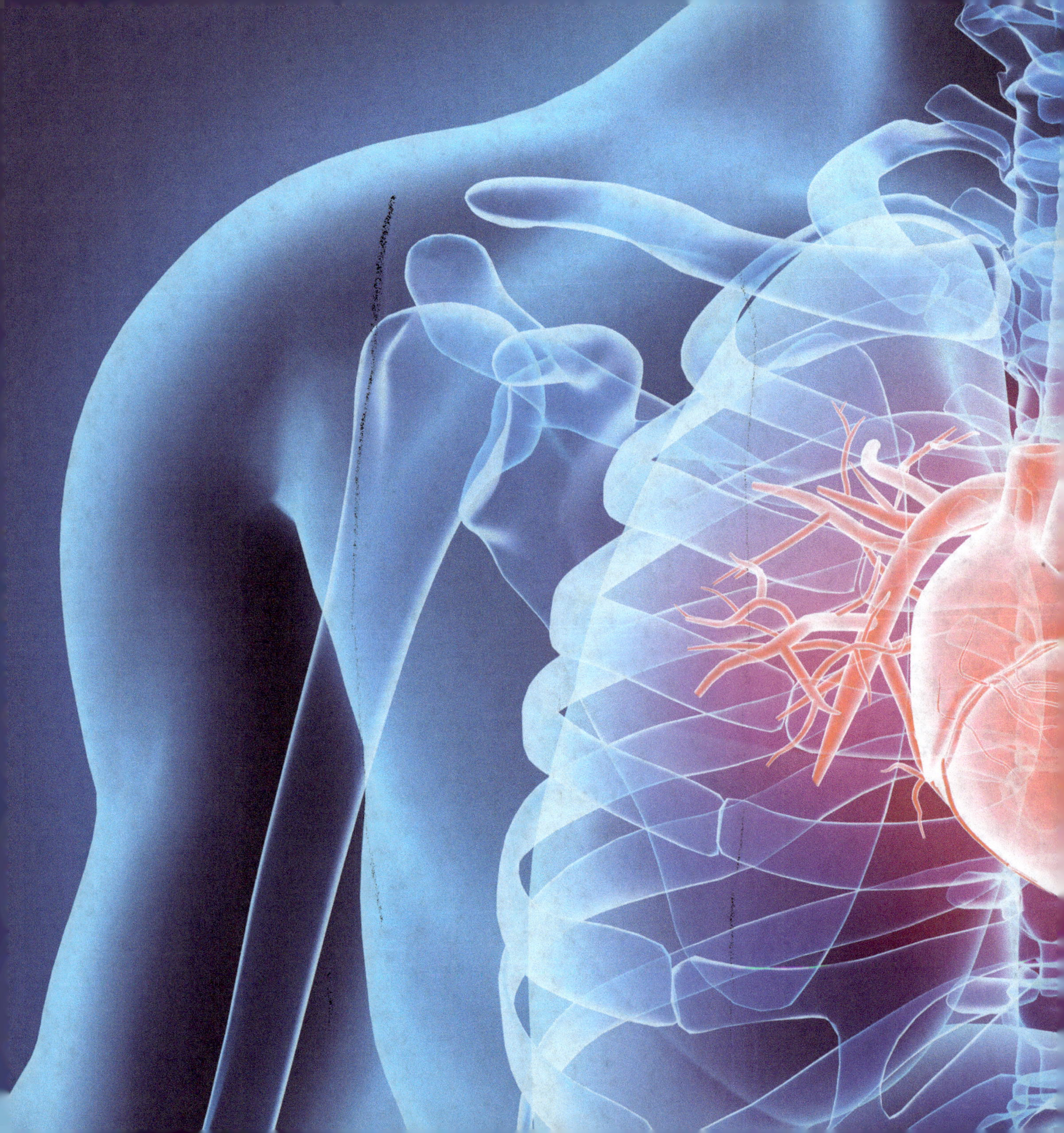

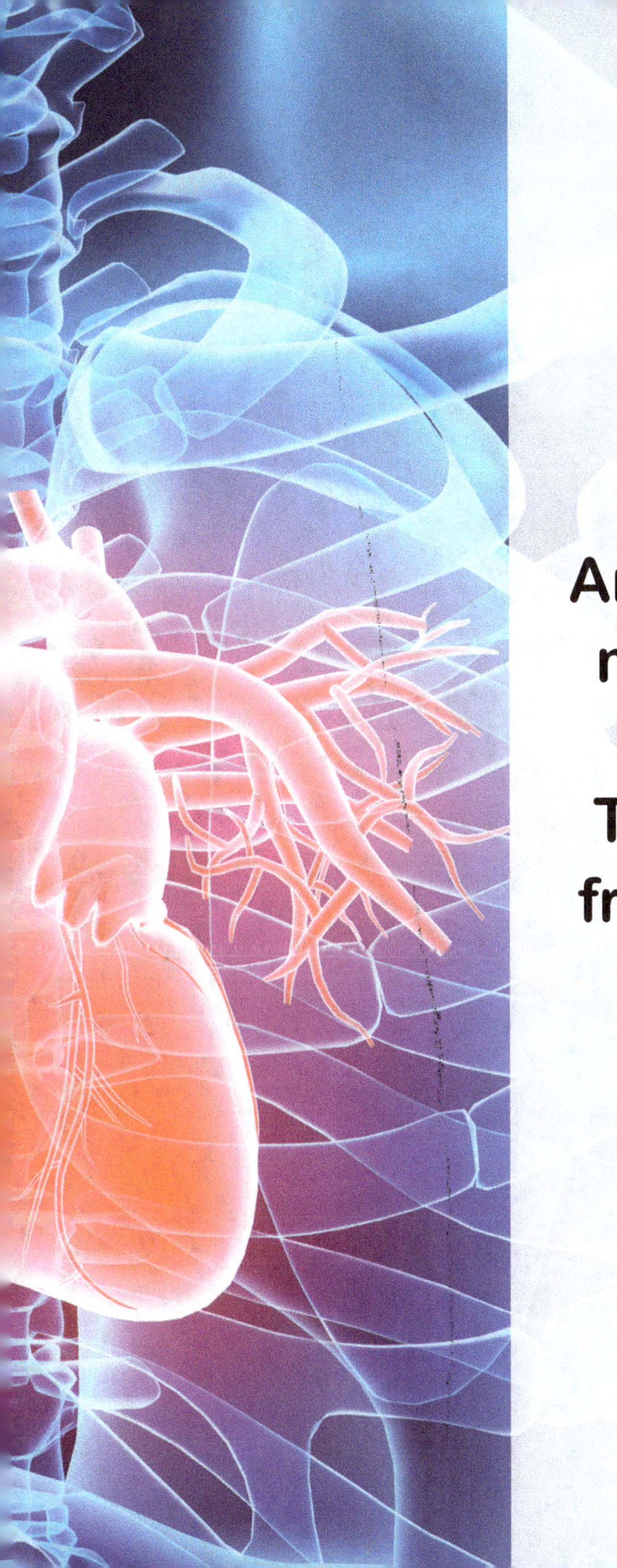

Arteries are the thickest muscular vessel in the body and are elastic. They carry blood away from our heart to all the tissues of our body.

Their elasticity helps
maintain our blood
pressure. The largest
artery in our body
is the aorta and it is
connected to the left
ventricle of our heart.

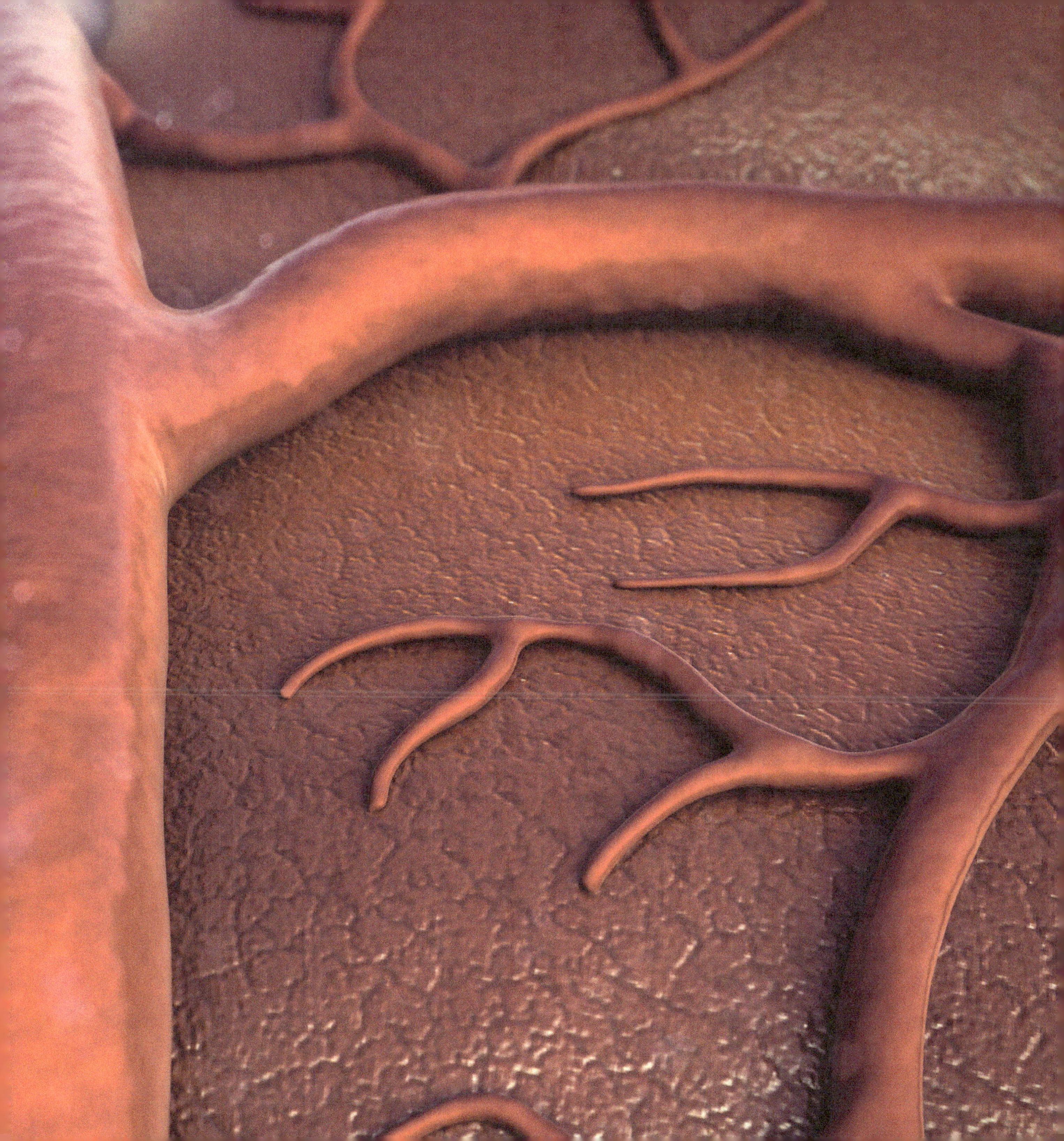

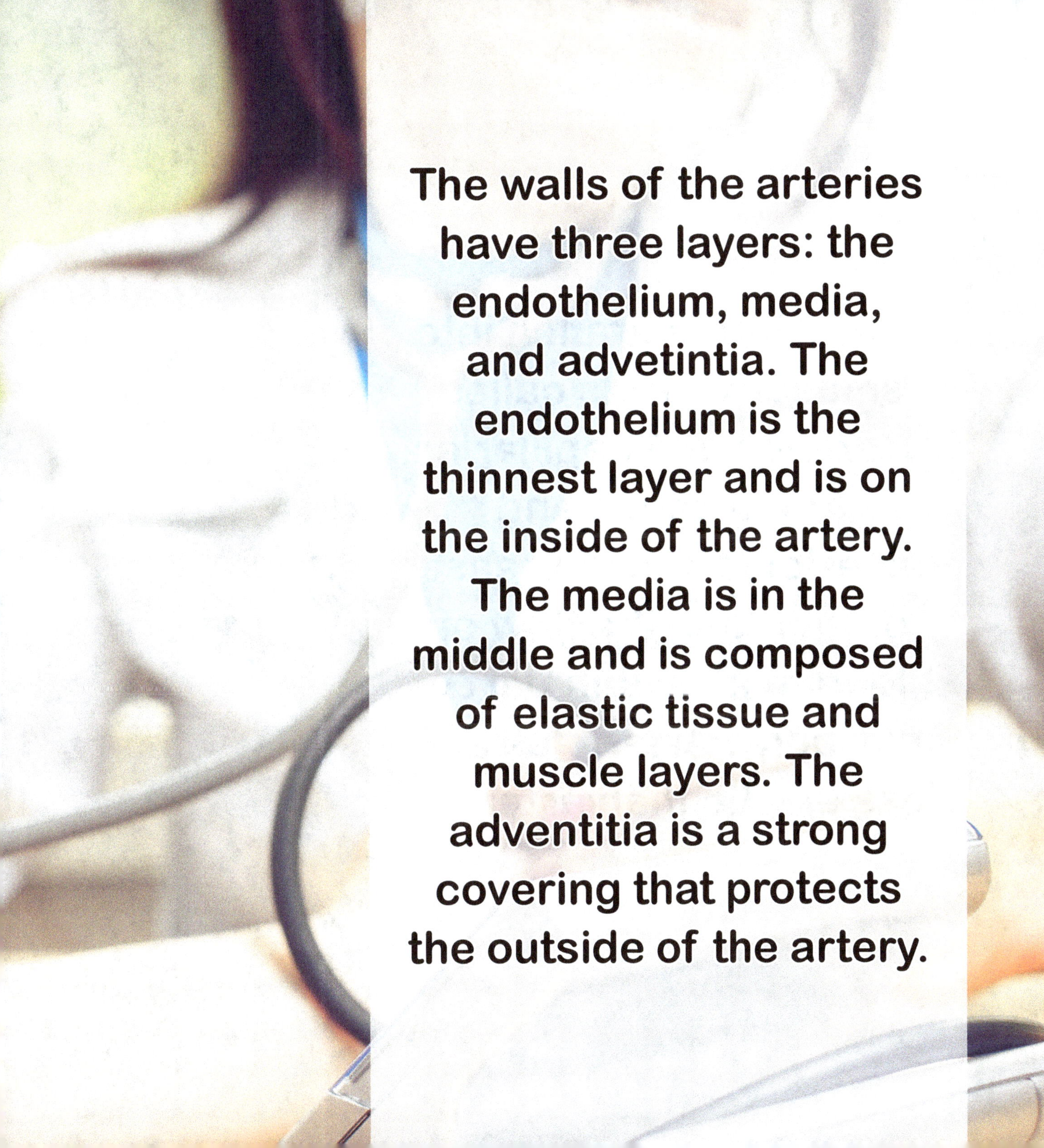

The walls of the arteries have three layers: the endothelium, media, and advetintia. The endothelium is the thinnest layer and is on the inside of the artery. The media is in the middle and is composed of elastic tissue and muscle layers. The adventitia is a strong covering that protects the outside of the artery.

Our arteries branch into smaller vessels called arterioles and capillaries. The arteries and arterioles can decrease or increase the flow of blood to a certain part of our body. Arterioles are less elastic than arteries.

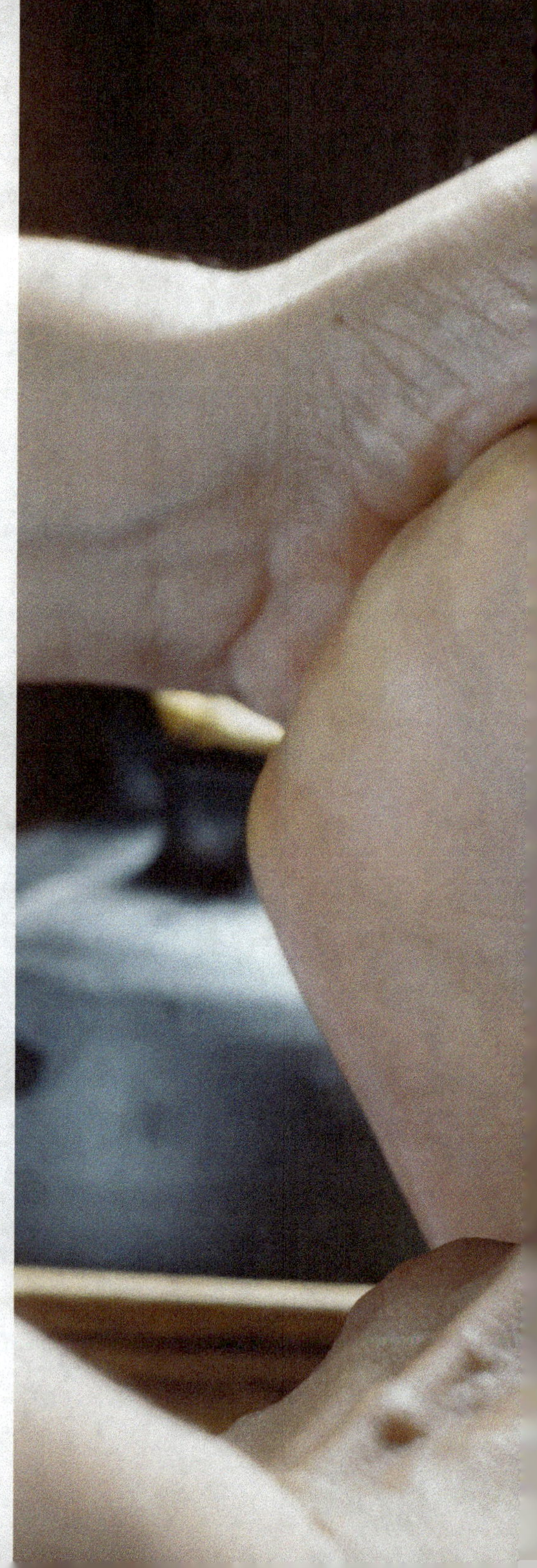

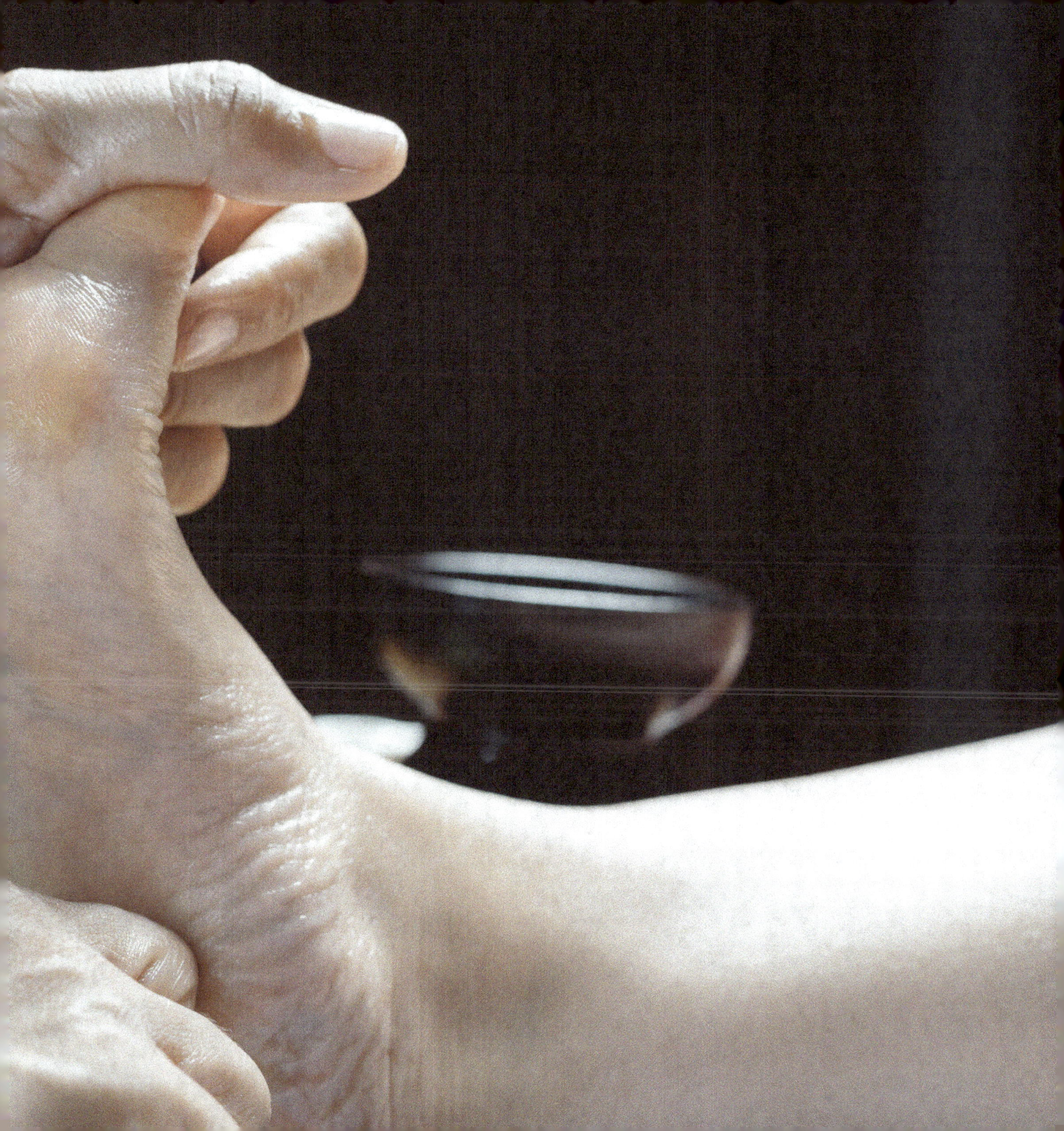

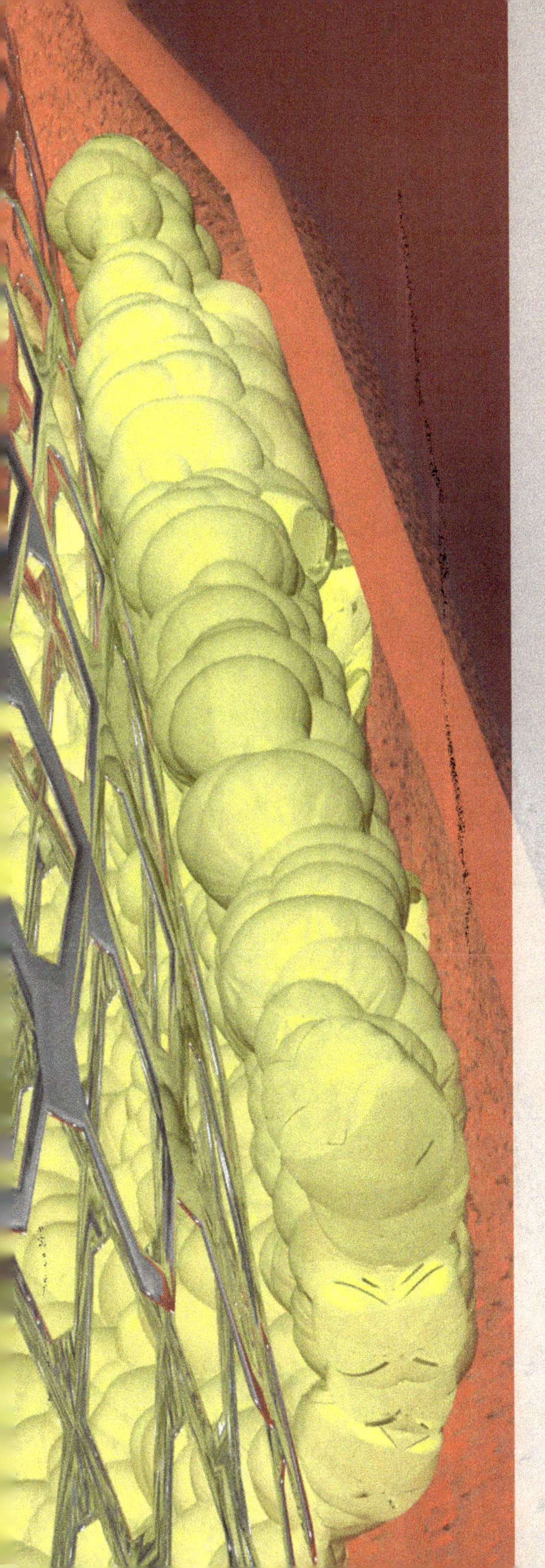

Veins, on the other hand, carry blood back to our heart. They aren't as thick as the arteries but they are responsible for preventing the blood from flowing backwards, using their valve structures.

Superior and inferior veins are the two largest veins in our body. The superior vein is located above the heart while the inferior vein is located below the heart.

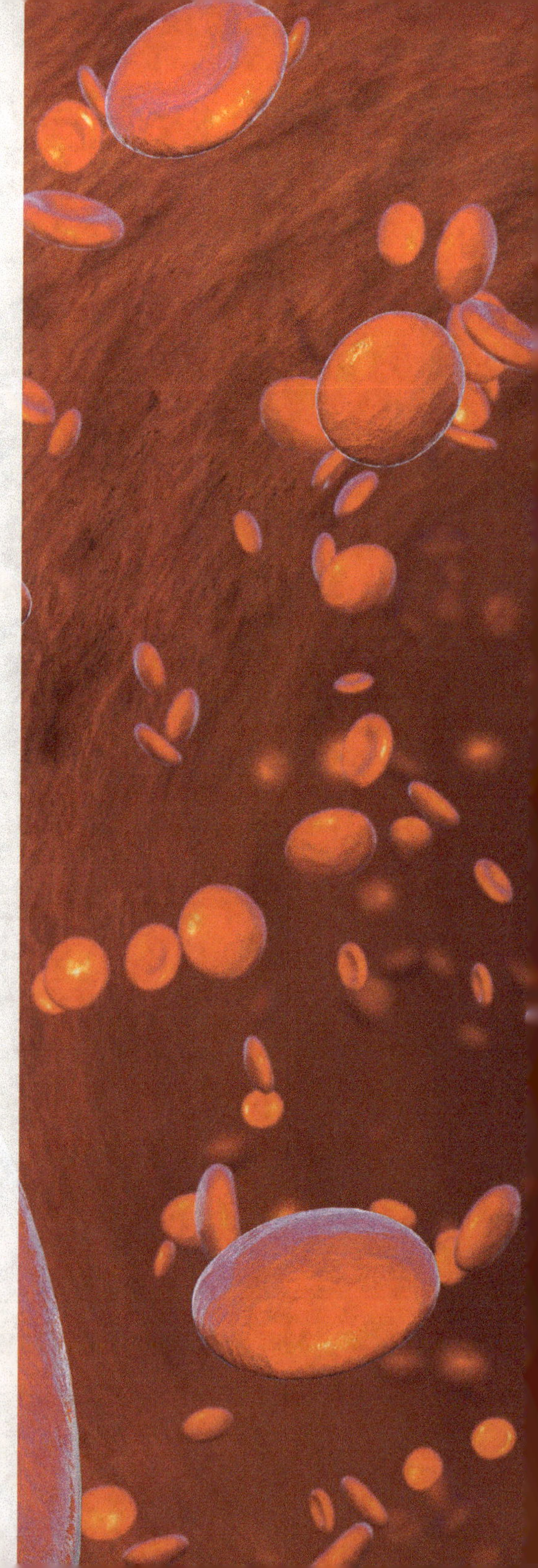

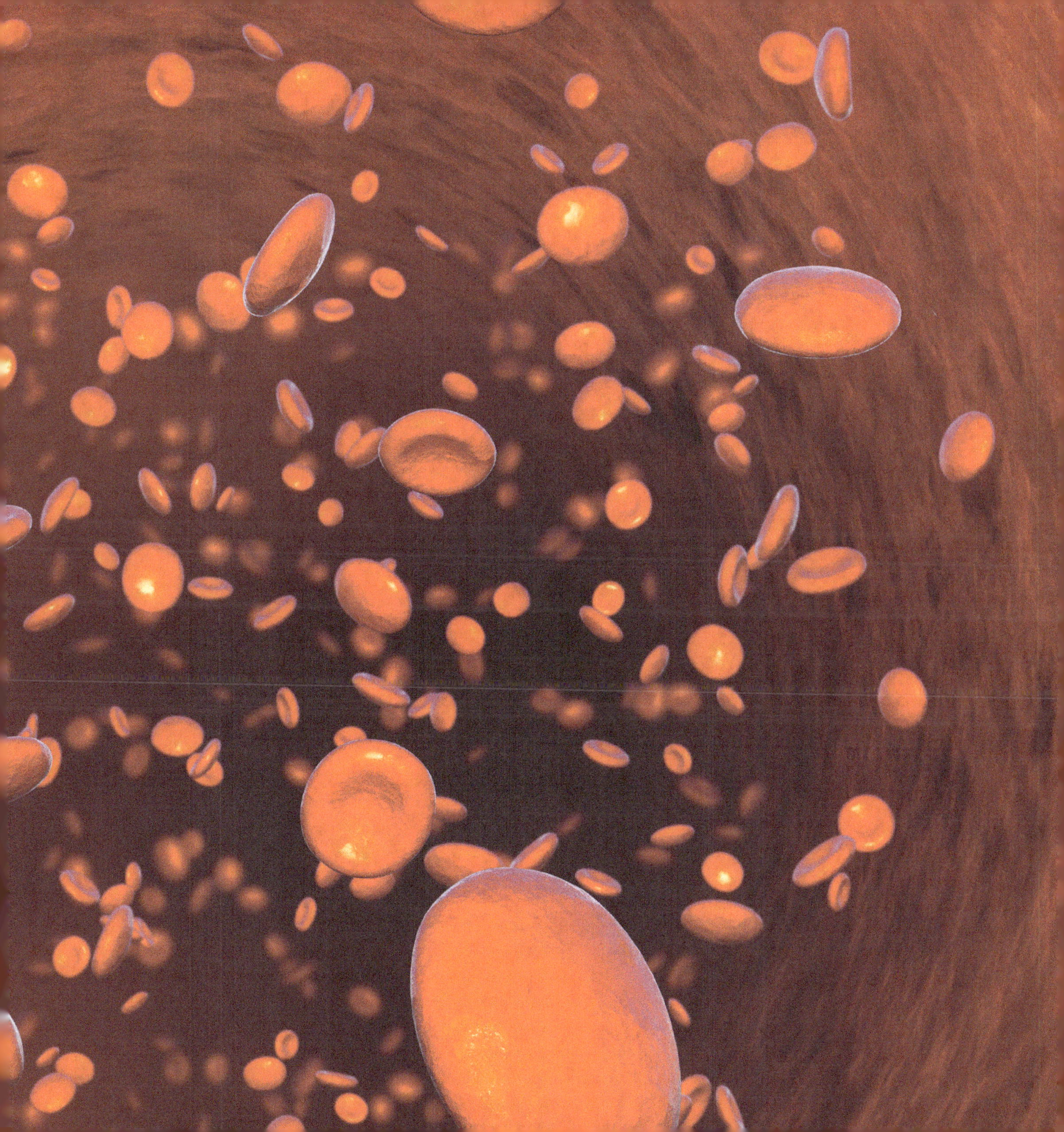

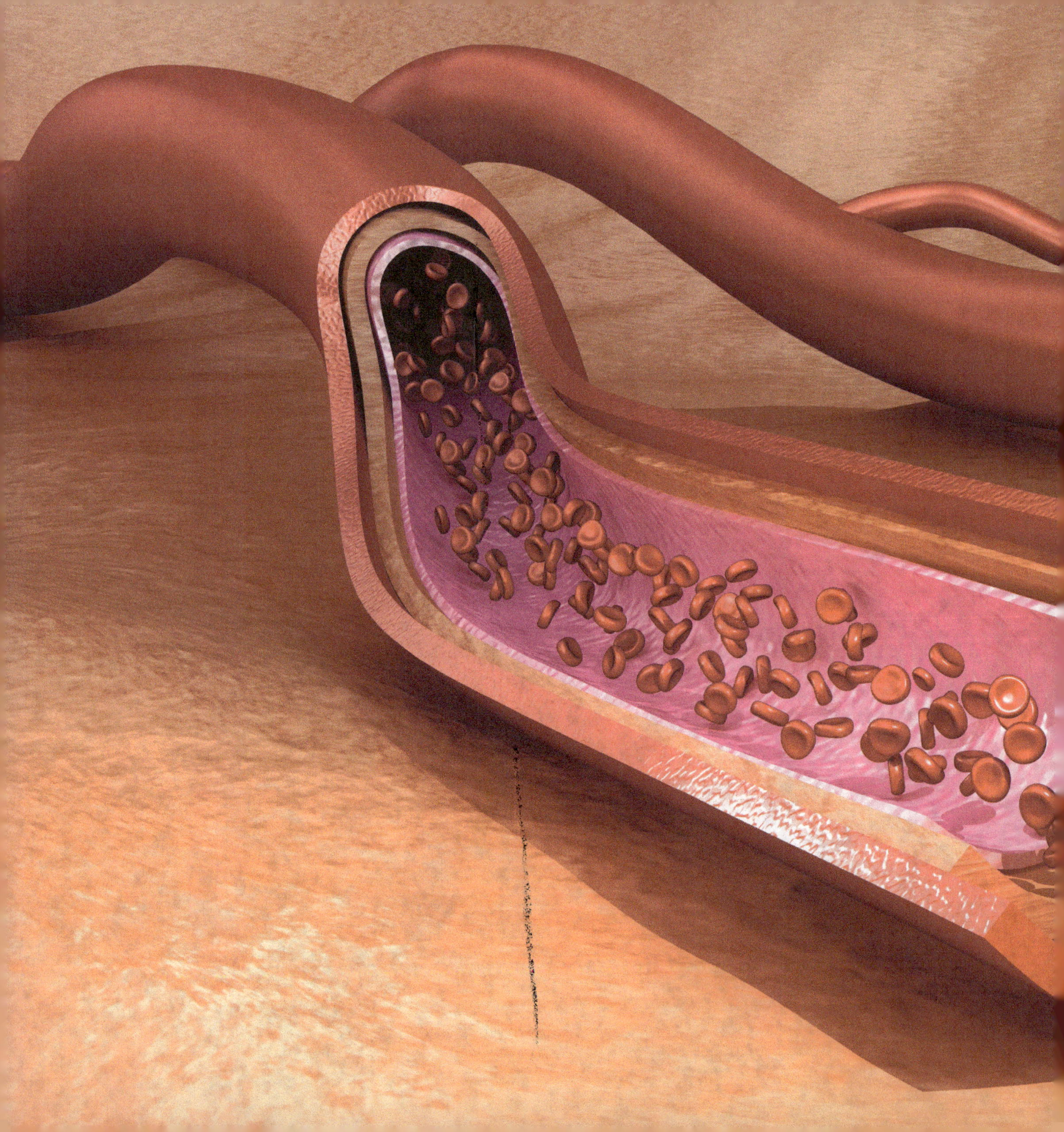

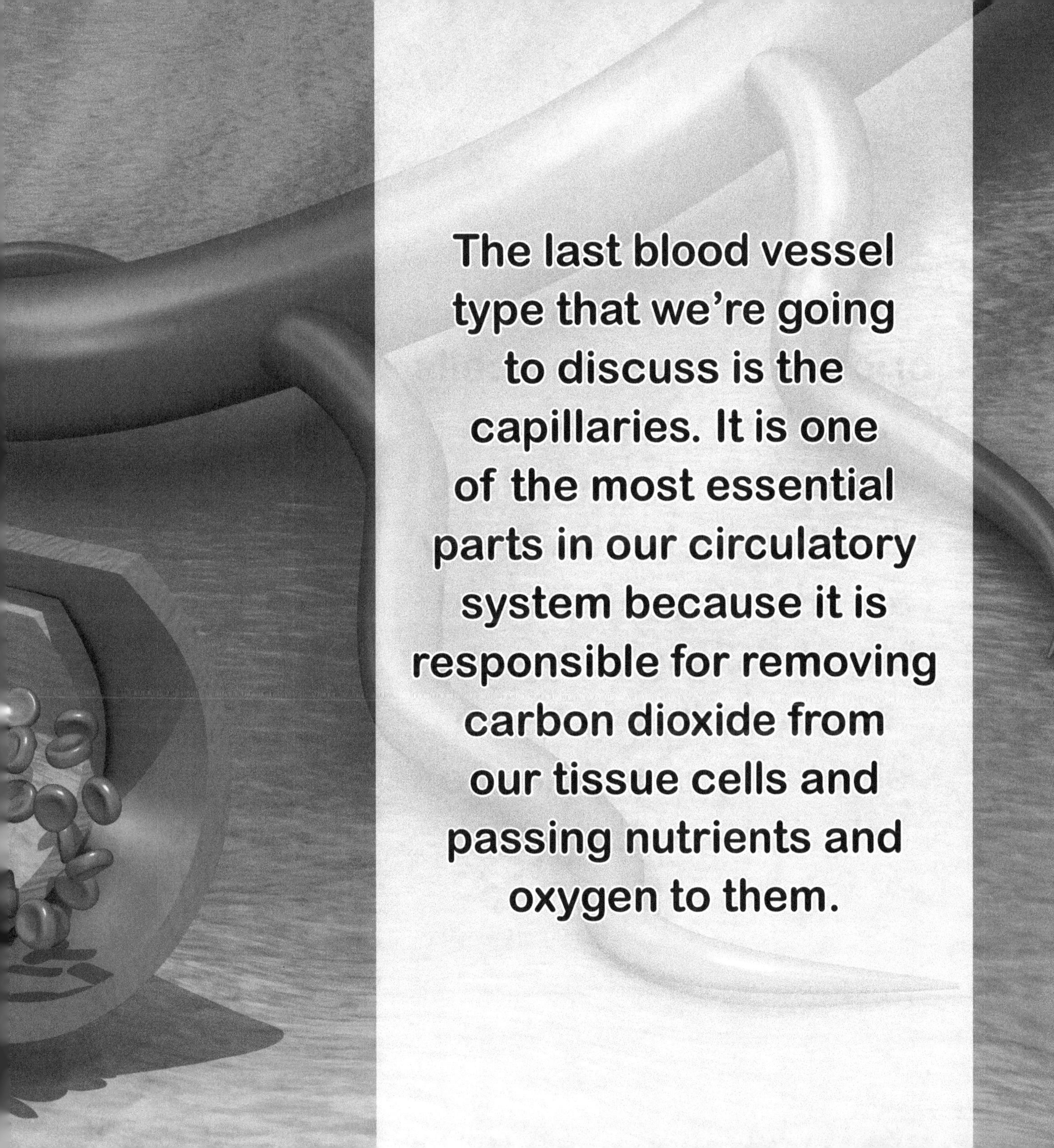
The last blood vessel
type that we're going
to discuss is the
capillaries. It is one
of the most essential
parts in our circulatory
system because it is
responsible for removing
carbon dioxide from
our tissue cells and
passing nutrients and
oxygen to them.

Capillaries act as a bridge between the cells and the arteries and veins. It is the smallest blood vessel in the body and the flow of the red blood cells is very slow because it only has a single layer, unlike the arteries and the veins.

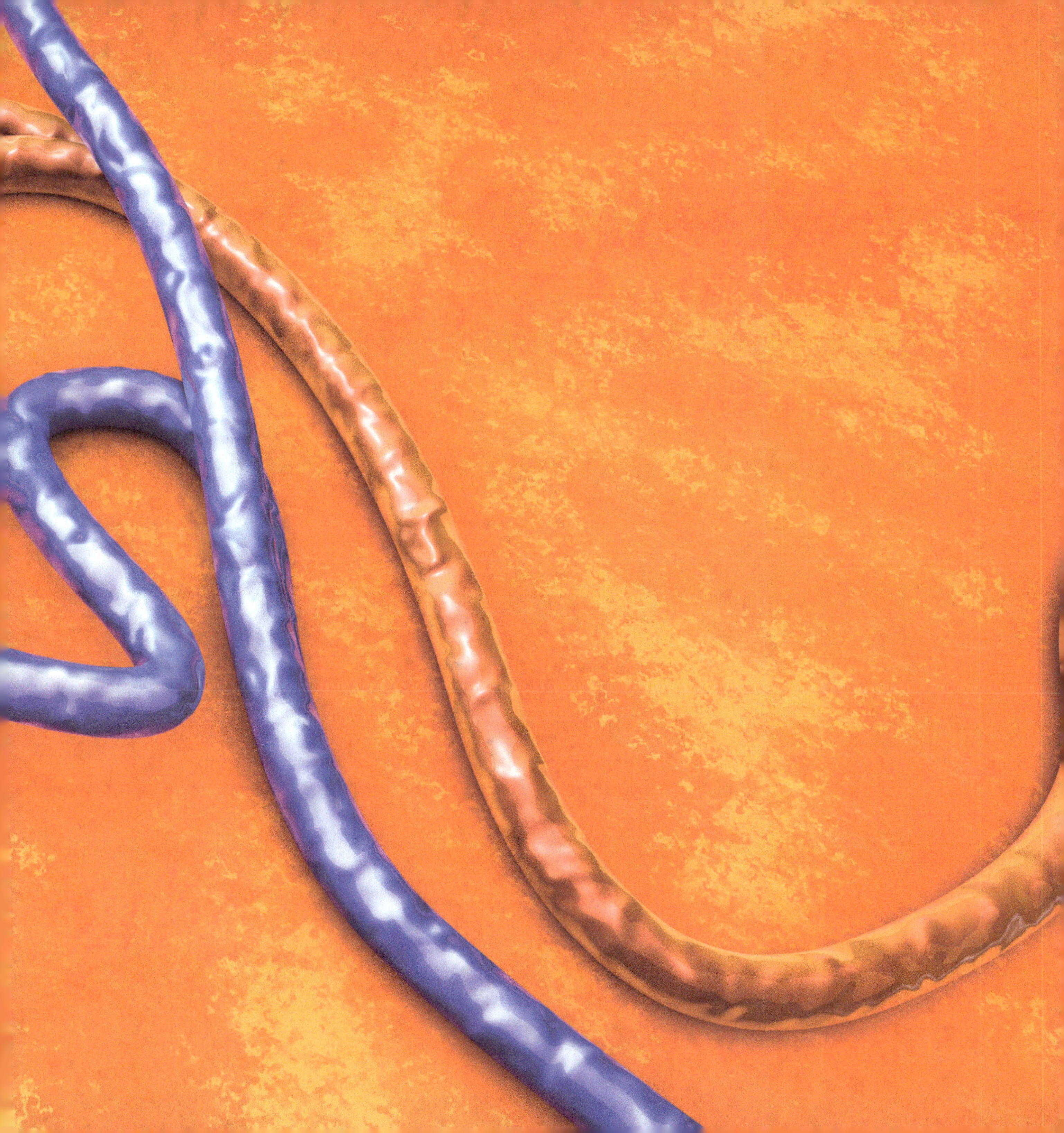

The circulation of blood in our body is essential for keeping our immune system and our heart healthy. Each cell in our body needs oxygen and nutrients. We can improve blood circulation by exercising, eating healthy foods, and drinking enough water.

There is more to know about our blood circulation. Research and have fun!

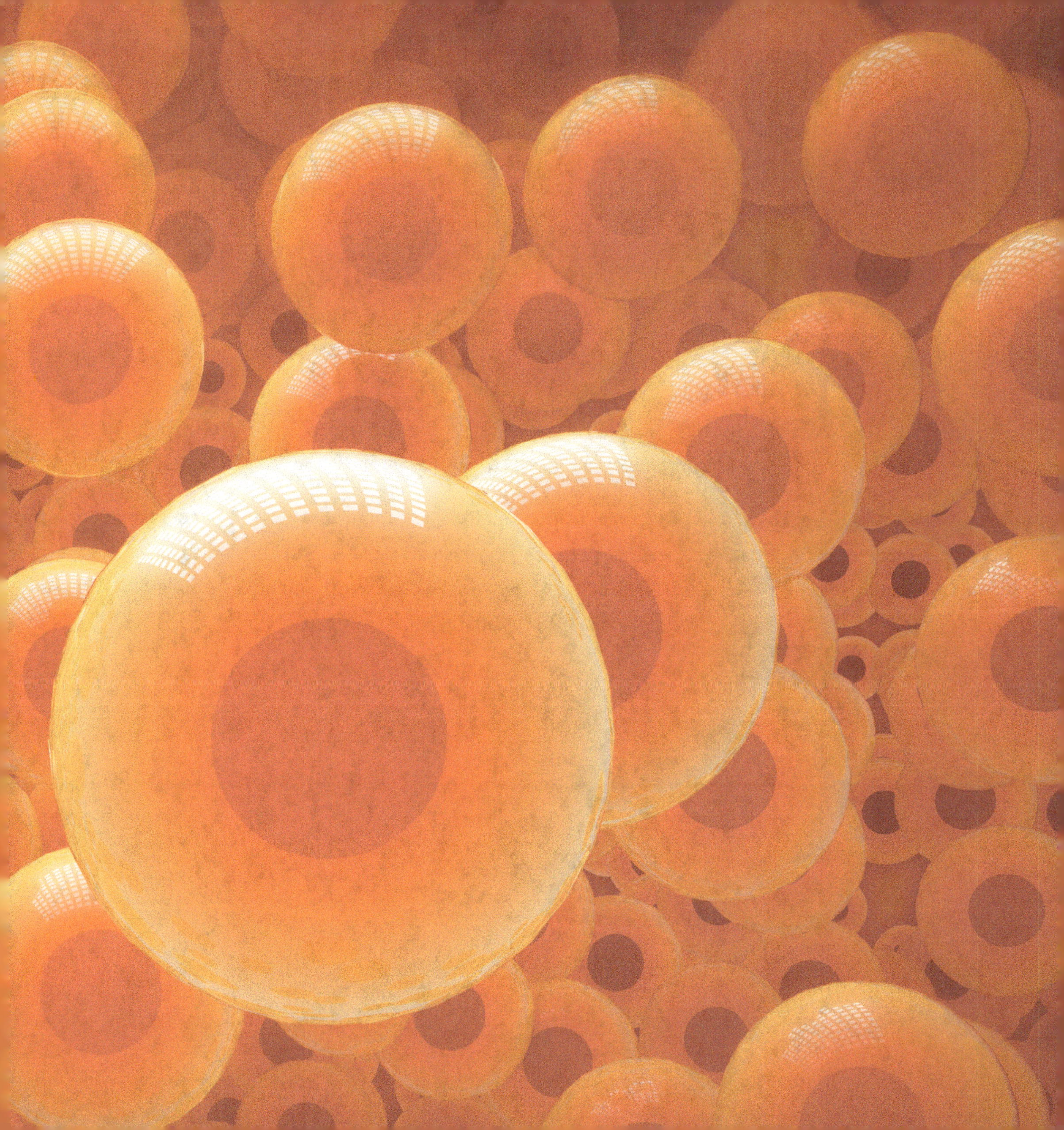

Visit
BABY PROFESSOR
EDUCATION KIDS
www.BabyProfessorBooks.com
to download Free Baby Professor eBooks
and view our catalog of new and exciting
Children's Books

9 798869 443410